The New Life

La vita nuova

The New Life

La vita nuova

A Dual-Language Book

Dante Alighieri

Edited and Translated by
STANLEY APPELBAUM

DOVER PUBLICATIONS
Garden City, New York

Bibliographical Note

This Dover edition, first published in 2006, is a complete republication of the Italian work originally published in Florence by Bartolomeo Sermatelli, together with a new English translation by Stanley Appelbaum, who also supplied the Introduction, the footnotes, and the Appendix of additional poems.

Library of Congress Cataloging-in-Publication Data

Dante Alighieri, 1265–1321.
    [Vita nuova. English & Italian]
    The new life = La vita nuova / Dante Alighieri ; edited and translated by Stanley Appelbaum.
        p. cm. — (Dual-language book)
    "A complete republication of the Italian work originally published in Florence by Bartolomeo Sermatelli, together with a new English translation . . . and Appendix of additional poems"—T.p. verso.
    ISBN-13: 978-0-486-45349-1 (pbk.)
    ISBN-10: 0-486-45349-9 (pbk.)
    I. Appelbaum, Stanley. II. Title. III. Title: Vita nuova. IV. Series.

PQ4315.58.A6 2006
851'.1—dc22

2006046328

Manufactured in the United States of America
45349910   2022
www.doverpublications.com

CONTENTS

INTRODUCTION

Dante Alighieri

Dante (short for Durante) Alighieri was born in Florence in the late spring of 1265. In the preceding century one ancestor had been a Knight Crusader, but the family was in humbler circumstances in the poet's day; his father may have been a moneylender. Dante's mother died when he was a child; his father remarried and begot more off-spring. The poet's early schooling couldn't have been anything exceptional, for it cost him great efforts when he began to catch up on his education as a young man. It was probably around the time of his father's death in 1283 that Dante married the well-connected Gemma Donati, to whom he had been betrothed since 1277.

In the 1280s he began writing lyric poetry, and by 1283 he was accepted into the fellowship of the established Florentine poets, whose chief, Guido Cavalcanti, about ten years older than he, became his best friend, according to Dante's own report in the *Vita nuova* (New Life). Dante may possibly have undertaken some desultory studies at the great university of Bologna in 1287. In 1289 he probably participated as a cavalryman in two Florentine victories over the hostile city-states of Arezzo and Pisa, Ghibelline strongholds.

Roughly speaking (because personal feuds also complicated the picture), the Ghibelline party stood for the supremacy of the Holy Roman Emperor in Italy over that of the pope, whose party was the Guelfs. The Florentine Guelfs, who had lost a major encounter in 1260, had driven out the Florentine Ghibellines definitively after the battle of Benevento in 1266. But Italian politics in Dante's time were so divisive that, at least by 1295, even the triumphant Florentine Guelfs had split drastically into two factions, the Whites (to whom Dante was to adhere) and the Blacks (headed by Corso Donati, a cousin of Dante's wife).

Dante's first major work, the *Vita nuova* (or *nova*), extensively dis-

cussed in the next section of this Introduction, was written between about 1293 and 1295. By that time Dante had clearly been studying hard on his own (it is unclear exactly when he received instruction from the well-traveled encyclopedic author and statesman Brunetto Latini, ca. 1220–1294, whom he was to place among the sodomites in the *Inferno*); presumably after the death in 1290 of the woman who had inspired the *Vita,* he had immersed himself in the Latin classics, theology, and philosophy (in its broadest medieval sense, including what we would call science).

By 1295 he was interested in politics (as a White) and took the necessary first step toward a political career in Florence: joining a craft guild (the most appropriate one for a poet and philosopher happened to be the guild of physicians and apothecaries). His career moved forward, reaching a peak in the period mid-June to mid-August 1300, when he served the normal two-month term as one of the six "priors" of his native city. It was during his term that his "best friend" Cavalcanti was exiled from Florence, dying later that year.

Now factional strife, propelled by pan-European events, was to close in on Dante. The Blacks, who had been exiled, joined the new alliance between the papacy and Charles de Valois, a French adventurer whose brother was Philip IV, king of France. When Dante was sent by his city government in 1301 as an emissary to the pope, he was detained in Rome, while Charles and the Blacks entered Florence; the poet would never see his home again. He refused to return when imperiously summoned by the vindictive Blacks, and he was sentenced to death in absentia. The banished Whites, constantly agitating to regain Florence, were finally crushed in battle in 1304, but Dante had already gone his own way as "a party of one." The remainder of his oeuvre was written in exile, including his last lyrics. (The *Rime* [Rhymes], aka the *Canzoniere* [Songbook], comprises those lyrics which he himself collected in the *Vita nuova* and the *Convivio,* as well as many other uncollected ones dating between the 1280s and the first decade of the fourteenth century; some of those contemporary with the *Vita* show him in a very different light: as a humorous carouser.)

For the rest of his life, until his death in Ravenna (probably from malaria) in 1321, Dante received hospitality at various North Italian courts outside of Tuscany, particularly with the Scala family in Verona. Between 1304 and 1307 (probably) he worked on the *Convivio* (Banquet), a learned work in which he anthologized his most learned *canzoni* (odes), claiming that the "compassionate lady" of the *Vita nuova,* whom he fell in love with after the death of his "most noble

lady," had actually been Lady Philosophy; it has been said that the *Convivio* (consisting of only four of a projected fifteen "books") was meant as his scholarly credentials for acceptance at foreign courts. During the same period he wrote the Latin prose treatise *De vulgari eloquentia* (On Vernacular Literature), completing one and a half books out of a possible four; in this work he defends the use of Italian (rather than Latin) for a wide range of subjects (in the *Vita nuova* he had restricted it to love lyrics), and champions a single, unified literary form of Italian. About 1313 he wrote another Latin prose monograph, *De monarchia* (On the Monarchy), now favoring the emperor over the pope. (Holy Roman Emperor Henry VII had marched into Northern Italy in 1310 to reclaim his predecessors' forfeited possession there, but, despite much urging from Dante and others, had remained largely inactive; he was carried off by a fever in 1313.)

Other Latin works of Dante's late years include thirteen prose epistles on a variety of subjects, two poetic eclogues, and a paper on hydrographics. (Two Italian-language poems attributed to him by a few scholars, the *Detto d'Amore* [Love's Discourse] and the *Fiore* [*Flower*; a paraphrase of parts of the *Roman de la Rose*], are naturally undated; if genuine, they were probably written before his exile.)

There was also to be one more work in Italian, fortunately completed not long before his death: the *Commedia* (called *Divina commedia* ever since the Venetian edition of 1555). This work, one of the supreme monuments of world literature, needs no further description here.[1] (Most scholars believe it was begun by 1307, but there are indications, mentioned below, in the *Vita nuova* that at least the germ of the idea for the *Commedia* was already present when the *Vita* was written in the early 1290s.)

The *Vita Nuova*

The *Vita nuova* was not published until 1576 (by Bartolomeo Sermatelli in Florence), but it was obviously fairly well known before that, since some forty manuscripts are extant.

"New Life" is the normal, and fully understandable, rendition of the work's title; some commentators, however, render *nuova* (or *nova*) as "young" and believe the title implies the record of the poet's youth.

---

1. About a third of it is fully translated (by the translator of the present volume), and the rest summarized, in the Dover dual-language book *The Divine Comedy: Selected Cantos* (2000; ISBN 0-486-41127-3).

(But in the usage of Dante and his contemporaries *novo* generally means "new" or even "amazing," while the words for young are *giovane* and *novello*.) The *Vita nuova*, which has been savaged by some critics in the past (along with all the rest of Dante's output before the *Commedia*) as being cold, cerebral, artificial, or even mincing, has generally found staunch champions and, though obviously less awe-inspiring than the *Commedia*, can be seen as the other pole of Dante's oeuvre, related to the *Commedia* in significant ways. It has also been called "one of the first important examples of Italian literary prose," and its most famous poem, "Tanto gentile . . . ," has been called "one of the most exquisite sonnets in all of world literature."

Because the *Vita* is the chief monument of a certain school of poetry, and because in it Dante mentions certain predecessors and contemporary poets, it may be helpful here to sketch the history of Italian vernacular poetry down to about 1300.

No doubt because Italy was the heartland of ancient Roman civilization, Italian took longer than other major Romance languages to assert its independence from Latin, and Italian literature made its appearance long after that of other West European lands.[2] The earliest surviving Italian poetry (minor examples of minstrelsy) date from about 1190, and the first major poem (which is very good indeed) is Saint Francis's famous "Canticle" of ca. 1225. In the first two thirds of the thirteenth century the Provençal influence on Italian poetry was immense[3] (Provençal poetry had preceded Italian by a good century). Not only did Provençal verse circulate in manuscript: Provençal poets in person flooded all parts of Italy after the southern French courts that had supported them were wiped out in the so-called Albigensian Crusade (wars, ostensibly religious and antiheretical, waged against the south between 1209 and 1249 by northern French rulers).

The first major school of Italian poetry was the Sicilian, presided over by the sybaritic Holy Roman Emperor Frederick II; its chief representative was Giacomo (or Jacopo) da (of/from) Lentini[4] (flourished 1215–1233), also called "the Notary"; it may have been Giacomo who developed the sonnet out of earlier song forms. After the Sicilian style had reached Tuscany, two of its chief exponents were Bonagiunta Orbicciani of Lucca (active in the 1240s and 1250s, possibly still active

---

2. Nor did Italian literature achieve until the fourteenth century (with the *Commedia*, Boccaccio, and Petrarch) the preeminence in Europe it was to enjoy until 1600 at least.   3. There are even eight lines in Provençal in the *Divina Commedia* (*Purgatorio* XXVI, 140–147)!   4. Lentini is in southeastern Sicily, between Catania and Siracusa.

in the 1270s) and Guittone d'Arezzo (of Arezzo; ca. 1230–1294). All these men wrote brief love lyrics, which Dante later came to consider as banal or puerile; he himself adhered to the next North Italian school.

This new fashion is named by literary historians after a phrase of Dante's own coinage: the *dolce stil nuovo* (or *novo*; the sweet new style). In canto XXIV of the *Purgatorio,* Dante meets Bonagiunta himself, who asks the otherworld traveler (quoting a line from the *Vita nuova*):

> "But tell me whether I see here the man who brought
>   forth the new style of poetry, beginning with
>   'Ladies who have an understanding of love.'"
> And I replied: "I am such a man that, what
>   Love inspires in me, I write down, and in the fashion
>   in which he dictates it within me, I express it."
> "O brother," he said, "now I see the obstacle
>   that kept the Notary, Guittone, and me
>   outside the sweet new style that I hear!
> I see clearly that your pens
>   follow closely behind the one who dictates to you,
>   which certainly was not the case with ours;
> and anyone who takes the trouble to investigate further
>   will see no other difference between one style and the other."

The lyric verse of the *dolce stil nuovo* was chiefly love poetry, interiorized and more psychological than allegorical, in which the woman being praised was "angelicized" and all but worshipped like the Blessed Virgin. (In earlier Provençal verse, imitated by the northern French *trouvères* and the German-language *Minnesänger,* the troubadours had generally pledged a secular sort of feudal service to a very human noblewoman.) In the *dolce stil nuovo* a special vocabulary of highly charged words was constantly repeated in a variety of combinations (for instance, *gentile* [noble, nice, kindly] connoted "of a nature capable of feeling genuine, loyal love"). The first great poet of the school, perhaps its originator, was Guido Guinizzelli (also spelled Guinizelli and Guinicelli) of Bologna (ca. 1230–1276); the subsequent leader of the school was Dante's Florentine friend Guido Cavalcanti, soon matched (though not in every critic's opinion) by Dante himself. (The *Vita nuova* is dedicated to Cavalcanti, written for him and in accordance with his advice.) Guinizzelli (or at least his authorial persona) tended to derive enjoyment from his poetic love affairs; not so,

Cavalcanti. Dante injected even more theology, metaphysics, and sundry lore into his own *dolce stil nuovo* compositions and, as mentioned above, erected the school's chief monument in the *Vita nuova* besides giving it its name in the *Commedia*.

In the *Vita nuova* Dante assembled a selection of his youthful poems within a prose framework that situates them in a chronological autobiographical context (which may not be strictly truthful, though incautious biographers are still taking most of his assertions at face value) and analyzes them (generally in a superficial, tedious way). The work includes twenty-five sonnets, one *ballata* (a form based on dance songs, often—though not here—featuring a refrain), and five *canzoni*,[5] one of them intentionally left incomplete and serving as a hinge between the second and third parts of the tripartite *Vita* (the first part ends after section XVII; the second, after section XXVII).

The prose-and-verse combination exemplified by the *Vita* is technically called a prosimetrum. This literary form goes back to classical Greco-Roman times, but the most influential example was the *De consolatione philosophiae* (On the Consolation Offered by Philosophy) by Boethius, written ca. 524 A.D. (the source of Dante's Lady Philosophy in the *Convivio*). Another prosimetrum influence, much closer in time, could have been the thirteenth-century Provençal *vidas* (lives),[6] largely baseless fictionalized biographies of long-dead troubadours whose surviving poems were naively ransacked for clues to the situations in which they were written.

Since the prose of the *Vita nuova* provides the interconnections of a series of love poems, it comprises a love story: an ardent but spiritualized, sublimated love for an ideal but inaccessible, married woman. The first part of the book records the beginnings and eventual consolidation of the one-sided romance; the second part contains high praises of the lady; she then dies, and the third and last part is consecrated to her memory. When not called by the name Beatrice (she who makes blessed; Florentine custom could shorten this to the much less ethereal Bice), this woman is referred to by the code phrases "my lady" and "that most noble lady." Possibly nonexistent (though the intensity of the poet's reactions, here and in the *Commedia*, make the reality of *some* crucial experience hard to deny),

---

5. *Canzone* translates naturally as "song," but, following certain authorities, it is translated in this Dover volume as "ode." In *De vulgari eloquentia* Dante calls this multistanza verse form the noblest of all.   6. There were also *razos* ("explanations" [of individual poems]).

and possibly a literary conflation of several women, she was later iden-
tified by Dante's son as Beatrice Portinari.

This "real Beatrice" (combining Dante's statements with other
sources) was born in 1266, the daughter of a prominent banker and
public benefactor. Around 1285 she married the banker Simone de'
Bardi, and she died on the evening of June 8, 1290. In the uncollected
Rime the figure of Beatrice (real or idolized) plays little part, and in
the *Convivio* it is Lady Philosophy that Dante extols (though he still
casts himself as the devotee of a divine woman), but in the *Commedia*
Beatrice returns in a supreme role. In canto II of the *Inferno* Vergil re-
lates that she was sent by the Blessed Virgin to activate him as Dante's
guide through the lower regions. When Dante emerges from
Purgatory (*Purgatorio* XXX), she replaces Vergil, reminding Dante of
his former love for her, which he has unworthily forgotten; she had set
his otherworld journey in motion to save his soul, because he had
gone astray after her death. In canto III of the *Paradiso* the poet calls
Beatrice "That sun which first warmed my breast with love." In
Paradiso XXXI she resumes her rightful place in the ranks of heaven,
replaced as Dante's guide by Saint Bernard.

Several features of the *Vita nuova* deserve special attention. One
very obvious one is its pervasive recourse to numerology: Dante as-
sociates with Beatrice the sacrosanct number nine (three Trinities;
the number of heavens; etc.) and brings that number into play with
uncomfortable frequency, sometimes in a distressingly far-fetched
way. (The *Commedia*, too, is numerological, being in three parts of
thirty-three cantos each, plus an introductory canto bringing the
total to the perfect number 100, ten tens.) Another feature that the
Vita shares with the *Commedia* (though to a much lesser degree) is
the scholarly periphrastic dating of events by astronomical phenom-
ena (in the Ptolemaic system, of course). Times of day are given in
canonical hours. Human physiology, especially mental perception, is
based on the belief in spirits that convey messages, moods, or
malaise from one part of the body to another. Scholastic terminology
is also frequent, e.g. essence, potentiality, substance, accident, form,
and matter.

The language is very involved, making use of countless conceits,
multiple negations in place of positive declarations, and a wide range
of other rhetorical devices. There is an outrageous example of folk et-
ymology in section XXIV. Biblical quotations, some of the speeches of
Love, and a few other phrases are given in Latin (which in the present
translation is rendered directly into English, right alongside the ren-

dering of the Italian: the facing pages of the original text will show clearly where the Latin occurs).

The digression in section XXV (already promised in section XII) is a particularly interesting bit of early-modern literary history and criticism (of course, literary criticism had already reached incomparably greater heights in Greco-Roman antiquity).

In addition to the links between the *Vita nuova* and the *Divina Commedia* already pointed out, there are many others which help justify the suggestion made above that they form the two strong poles, early and late, of a magnificent oeuvre. Not only are both works carefully structured, in three parts; not only is the *Vita* referred to in the *Commedia* (and one of its poems with particular pride); not only are they both (literally) visionary works: it is hard not to believe that Dante's vow, at the very end of the *Vita*, to create something unique in Beatrice's honor is somehow connected with his later magnum opus. Furthermore, lines in the ode in *Vita* XIX refer to "a man who expects to lose her/and who will say in the Inferno: 'O souls of the damned,/I have seen the hope of the souls in bliss.'" All in all, the belittling of the *Vita nuova* is, or should be, a thing of the past.

The Appendix to This Volume

This Dover volume is enriched by the inclusion (also in dual-language format) of seven brief poems that will shed light on some statements made above, and will help to illustrate the course of thirteenth-century Italian poetry. There is one poem each by Giacomo da Lentini, Bonagiunta, Guittone, and the two Guidos, Guinizzelli and Cavalcanti. In addition, there are two sonnets from Dante's *Rime* which are as different from the *Vita nuova* as can be, though they, too, date from well before his exile from Florence. (No *Rime* numbering is given for these two poems, because the numbering varies in different editions.)

In the first, in which Dante addresses Cavalcanti, he also mentions: their poetic crony Lapo Gianni (ca. 1270–ca. 1332), Vanna (probably the sweetheart of Cavalcanti discussed in *Vita* XXIV), Lagia (another sweetheart in the coterie), and "lady number thirty" (no doubt, a reference to the poetic list of sixty Florentine beauties referred to in *Vita* VI).

The second sonnet by Dante in the Appendix is part of a running poetic feud, or scurrilous slanging match, with Forese Donati, brother

of Corso and cousin of Gemma, Dante's wife. It has been dated to ca. 1295, the period of Dante's "going astray" after Beatrice's death. "Bicci" was a nickname of Forese's. The last three lines hint at unsavory doings, probably wife swapping. In addition, Dante, far from being mealymouthed here, takes the name of the Lord in vain, to say the least!

The New Life
La vita nuova

I. In quella parte del libro de la mia memoria dinanzi a la quale poco si potrebbe leggere, si trova una rubrica la quale dice: *Incipit vita nova*. Sotto la quale rubrica io trovo scritte le parole le quali è mio intendimento d'assemplare in questo libello; e se non tutte, almeno la loro sentenzia.

II. Nove fiate già appresso lo mio nascimento era tornato lo cielo de la luce quasi a uno medesimo punto, quanto a la sua propria girazione, quando a li miei occhi apparve prima la gloriosa donna de la mia mente, la quale fu chiamata da molti Beatrice li quali non sapeano che si chiamare. Ella era in questa vita già stata tanto, che ne lo suo tempo lo cielo stellato era mosso verso la parte d'oriente de le dodici parti l'una d'un grado, sì che quasi dal principio del suo anno nono apparve a me, ed io la vidi quasi da la fine del mio nono. Apparve vestita di nobilissimo colore, umile e onesto, sanguigno, cinta e ornata a la guisa che a la sua giovanissima etade si convenia. In quello punto dico veracemente che lo spirito de la vita, lo quale dimora ne la secretissima camera de lo cuore, cominciò a tremare sì fortemente, che apparia ne li menimi polsi orribilmente; e tremando disse queste parole: «Ecce deus fortior me, qui veniens dominabitur michi». In quello punto lo spirito animale, lo quale dimora ne l'alta camera ne la quale tutti li spiriti sensitivi portano le loro percezioni, si cominciò a maravigliare molto, e parlando spezialmente a li spiriti del viso, sì disse queste parole: «Apparuit iam beatitudo vestra». In quello punto lo spirito naturale, lo quale dimora in quella parte ove si ministra lo nutrimento nostro, cominciò a piangere, e piangendo disse queste parole: «Heu miser, quia frequenter impeditus ero deinceps!» D'allora innanzi dico che Amore segnoreggiò la mia anima, la quale fu sì tosto a lui disponsata, e cominciò a prendere sopra me tanta sicurtade e tanta signoria per la vertù che li dava la mia imaginazione, che me convenia fare tutti li suoi piaceri compiutamente. Elli mi comandava molte volte che io cercasse per vedere questa angiola giovanissima;

I. In that part of the book of my memory before which little may be read is found a rubric which says: "The new life begins." Below this rubric I find written the words which it is my intention to transcribe into this little book: if not all of them, at least their gist.

II. By now, nine times after my birth the heaven of light[1] had nearly returned to the same point in its own revolutions, when there first appeared to my eyes the glorious lady of my mind, who was called Beatrice by many who did not know how rightly to name her. She had already been so long in this life that in her time the heaven of fixed stars[2] had moved eastward one of the twelve parts of a degree,[3] so that she appeared to me when she was nearly at the outset of her ninth year, and I saw her when nearly at the end of my ninth. She appeared clad in a most noble color, humble and modest, blood-red, girdled and adorned in the manner befitting her very tender years. At that moment, I say truly, the vital spirit, which resides in the most secret chamber of the heart, began to tremble so strongly that it was terribly evident in my slightest heartbeats, and tremblingly it spoke these words: "Behold a god stronger than I, who is coming and will dominate me." At that moment, the animate spirit, which resides in the lofty chamber to which all the sensory spirits convey their perceptions,[4] began to marvel greatly and, addressing the spirits of sight in particular, spoke these words: "Your bliss has already appeared." At that moment, the natural spirit, which resides in that organ where our nutriment is regulated,[5] began to weep, and tearfully spoke these words: "Woe is me, for I shall be frequently hindered henceforth!" From then on, I say, Love tyrannized over my soul, which was so quickly wedded to him, and he began to assume so much assurance and tyranny over me, by the power my imagination lent him, that it behooved me to satisfy all his wishes completely. Many a time he commanded me to try and see that very young angel; so that in my boyhood I often went in quest of her, and saw her to be of such noble and

---

1. The sun (the fourth of the nine concentric heavens in medieval astronomy); each revolution, of course, is a year. 2. The eighth. 3. The stars were deemed to move one "degree" in a century, so that Beatrice had lived one-twelfth of that time; that is, she was over eight. 4. The brain. 5. The liver.

3

onde io ne la mia puerizia molte volte l'andai cercando, e vedeala di sì nobili e laudabili portamenti, che certo di lei si potea dire quella parola del poeta Omero: «Ella non parea figliuola d'uomo mortale, ma di deo». E avvegna che la sua imagine, la quale continuatamente meco stava, fosse baldanza d'Amore a segnoreggiare me, tuttavia era di sì nobilissima vertù, che nulla volta sofferse che Amore mi reggesse sanza lo fedele consiglio de la ragione in quelle cose là ove cotale consiglio fosse utile a udire. E però che soprastare a le passioni e atti di tanta gioventudine pare alcuno parlare fabuloso, mi partirò da esse; e trapassando molte cose le quali si potrebbero trarre de l'essemplo onde nascono queste, verrò a quelle parole le quali sono scritte ne la mia memoria sotto maggiori paragrafi.

III. Poi che fuoro passati tanti die, che appunto erano compiuti li nove anni appresso l'apparimento soprascritto di questa gentilissima, ne l'ultimo di questi die avvenne che questa mirabile donna apparve a me vestita di colore bianchissimo, in mezzo a due gentili donne, le quali erano di più lunga etade; e passando per una via, volse li occhi verso quella parte ov'io era molto pauroso, e per la sua ineffabile cortesia, la quale è oggi meritata nel grande secolo, mi salutoe molto virtuosamente, tanto che me parve allora vedere tutti li termini de la beatitudine. L'ora che lo suo dolcissimo salutare mi giunse, era fermamente nona di quello giorno; e però che quella fu la prima volta che le sue parole si mossero per venire a li miei orecchi, presi tanta dolcezza, che come inebriato mi partio da le genti, e ricorsi a lo solingo luogo d'una mia camera, e puosimi a pensare di questa cortesissima. E pensando di lei, mi sopragiunse uno soave sonno, ne lo quale m'apparve una maravigliosa visione: che me parea vedere ne la mia camera una nebula di colore di fuoco, dentro a la quale io discernea una figura d'uno segnore di pauroso aspetto a chi la guardasse; e pareami con tanta letizia, quanto a sè, che mirabile cosa era; e ne le sue parole dicea molte cose, le quali io non intendea se non poche; tra le quali intendea queste: «Ego dominus tuus». Ne le sue braccia mi parea vedere una persona dormire nuda, salvo che involta mi parea in uno drappo sanguigno leggeramente; la quale io riguardando molto intentivamente, conobbi ch'era la donna de la salute, la quale m'avea lo giorno dinanzi degnato di salutare. E ne l'una de le mani mi parea che questi tenesse una cosa la quale ardesse tutta, e pareami che mi dicesse queste parole: «Vide cor tuum». E quando elli era stato

praiseworthy behavior that that saying of the poet Homer could certainly be applied to her: "She seemed like the daughter not of a mortal man, but of a god."[6] And although her image, which was constantly with me, was a bold ploy of Love in order to dominate me, nevertheless it was of such noble force that it never allowed Love to rule me without the loyal advice of reason in matters where such advice might be usefully heard. And because dwelling on the passions and actions of so young a person seems like some recounting of fables, I shall drop this subject; and, omitting many things which could be inferred from the text which is the source of these words, I shall arrive at those words which are written in my memory under more important headings.

III. After so many days had passed that nine years exactly had elapsed since the aforesaid appearance of that most noble girl, on the last of these days it befell that that wonderful lady appeared to me clad in a dazzlingly white gown, walking between two gentlewomen, who were older than she. As she passed down a street, she turned her eyes toward where I was standing in great fear, and with her ineffable courtesy, which is today rewarded in the eternal life, she greeted me very virtuously, so that it seemed to me then that I was viewing every facet of bliss. The hour when her most sweet greeting came to me was precisely the ninth[7] of that day; and because that was the first time her words reached my ears, I was so delighted that I retired, as if intoxicated, from those I was with and withdrew to the loneliness of one of my rooms, where I set myself thinking upon that most courteous lady. And while thinking of her, I was overcome by a gentle slumber, in which a marvelous vision appeared to me: I thought I saw in my room a fiery-colored cloud within which I could make out the figure of a man of fearsome aspect to whoever beheld him; and he appeared so joyful personally that it was a wonder to behold; and in his words he said many things, only a few of which I understood; among them I understood this: "I am your master." In his arms I thought I saw a sleeping person who was nude except that she seemed to be loosely wrapped in a blood-red cloth; looking at her very closely, I recognized her as the lady of the salutary greeting who had deigned to greet me the day before. And I thought the man held in one hand something all ablaze, and I thought he spoke these words to me: "Behold your heart." And after

---

6. A reference to *Iliad* XXIV, 258, or *Odyssey* VI, 149, or both.   7. Probably 3 P.M., the ninth canonical hour, or nones.

alquanto, pareami che disvegliasse questa che dormia; e tanto si
sforzava per suo ingegno, che le facea mangiare questa cosa che in
mano li ardea, la quale ella mangiava dubitosamente. Appresso ciò
poco dimorava che la sua letizia si convertia in amarissimo pianto; e
così piangendo, si ricogliea questa donna ne le sue braccia, e con essa
mi parea che si ne gisse verso lo cielo; onde io sostenea sì grande an-
goscia, che lo mio deboletto sonno non poteo sostenere, anzi si ruppe
e fui disvegliato. E mantenente cominciai a pensare, e trovai che l'ora
ne la quale m'era questa visione apparita, era la quarta de la notte
stata; sì che appare manifestamente ch'ella fue la prima ora de le nove
ultime ore de la notte. Pensando io a ciò che m'era apparuto, pro-
puosi di farlo sentire a molti li quali erano famosi trovatori in quello
tempo: e con ciò fosse cosa che io avesse già veduto per me medesimo
l'arte del dire parole per rima, propuosi di fare uno sonetto, ne lo
quale io salutasse tutti li fedeli d'Amore; e pregandoli che giudicassero
la mia visione, scrissi a loro ciò che io avea nel mio sonno veduto. E
cominciai allora questo sonetto, lo quale comincia: A ciascun'alma
presa.

> A ciascun'alma presa e gentil core
>   nel cui cospetto ven lo dir presente,
>   in ciò che mi rescrivan suo parvente,
>   salute in lor segnor, cioè Amore.
> Già eran quasi che atterzate l'ore
>   del tempo che onne stella n'è lucente,
>   quando m'apparve Amor subitamente,
>   cui essenza membrar mi dà orrore.
> Allegro mi sembrava Amor tenendo
>   meo core in mano, e ne le braccia avea
>   madonna involta in un drappo dormendo.
> Poi la svegliava, e d'esto core ardendo
>   lei paventosa umilmente pascea:
>   appresso gir lo ne vedea piangendo.

Questo sonetto si divide in due parti; che ne la prima parte saluto e
domando risponsione, ne la seconda significo a che si dee rispondere.
La seconda parte comincia quivi: Già eran.
    A questo sonetto fue risposto da molti e di diverse sentenzie; tra li
quali fue risponditore quelli cui io chiamo primo de li miei amici, e
disse allora uno sonetto, lo quale comincia: Vedeste, al mio parere,

he had been there a while, I thought he awakened the sleeping woman; and he made such efforts of mind that he caused her to eat that object which was burning in his hand, which she ate hesitantly. Not long after that, his joy changed to most bitter weeping; and as he wept thus, that woman took shelter in his arms, and I thought he arose toward the sky with her; this caused me such anguish that I was unable to continue my light slumber; on the contrary, it was broken and I was awakened. And at once I began to think, and I found that the hour when that vision had appeared to me had been the fourth hour of the night;[8] so that it is clearly evident that it was the first hour of the last nine hours of nighttime. Pondering on the vision that had appeared to me, I determined to communicate it to many who were famous poets at that time; and inasmuch as I had already discovered in myself the art of setting words in verse, I resolved to make a sonnet in which I would greet all devotees of Love; and asking them to judge of my vision, I wrote to them what I had seen in my slumber. And I then began this sonnet, which begins: "To every captive soul."

> To every captive soul and truly loving heart
>   before whose eyes the present words arrive,
>   so that they write back their opinion to me:
>   greetings in the name of their master, Love.
>   Nearly a third of the hours had passed
>   of the time when every star shines,
>   when Love suddenly appeared to me,
>   the memory of whose aspect terrifies me.
> Love seemed merry to me as he held
>   my heart in his hand, and in his arms he had
>   my lady, asleep, enveloped in a cloth.
>   Then he awakened her, and of that burning heart
>   in fear she humbly partook:
>   afterward I saw him depart in tears.

This sonnet is divided into two parts; in the first part I send greetings and request a reply; in the second, I state what is to be replied to. The second part begins with the words "Nearly a third."

This sonnet was replied to by many, whose opinions differed; among those who replied was the man I call the foremost of my friends,[9] who then wrote the sonnet that begins "In my opinion, you

---

8. This has been glossed as the hour between 9 and 10 P.M.   9. Guido Cavalcanti.

onne valore. E questo fue quasi lo principio de l'amistà tra lui e me, quando elli seppe che io era quelli che li avea ciò mandato. Lo verace giudicio del detto sogno non fue veduto allora per alcuno, ma ora è manifestissimo a li più semplici.

IV. Da questa visione innanzi cominciò lo mio spirito naturale ad essere impedito ne la sua operazione, però che l'anima era tutta data nel pensare di questa gentilissima; onde io divenni in picciolo tempo poi di sì fraile e debole condizione, che a molti amici pesava de la mia vista; e molti pieni d'invidia già si procacciavano di sapere di me quello che io volea del tutto celare ad altrui. Ed io, accorgendomi del malvagio domandare che mi faceano, per la volontade d'Amore, lo quale mi comandava secondo lo consiglio de la ragione, rispondea loro che Amore era quelli che così m'avea governato. Dicea d'Amore, però che io portava nel viso tante de le sue insegne, che questo non si potea ricovrire. E quando mi domandavano «Per cui t'ha così distrutto questo Amore?», ed io sorridendo li guardava, e nulla dicea loro.

V. Uno giorno avvenne che questa gentilissima sedea in parte ove s'udiano parole de la regina de la gloria, ed io era in luogo dal quale vedea la mia beatitudine; e nel mezzo di lei e di me per la retta linea sedea una gentile donna di molto piacevole aspetto, la quale mi mirava spesse volte, maravigliandosi del mio sguardare, che parea che sopra lei terminasse. Onde molti s'accorsero de lo suo mirare; e in tanto vi fue posto mente, che, partendomi da questo luogo, mi sentio dicere appresso di me: «Vedi come cotale donna distrugge la persona di costui»; e nominandola, io intesi che dicea di colei che mezzo era stata ne la linea retta che movea da la gentilissima Beatrice e terminava ne li occhi miei. Allora mi confortai molto, assicurandomi che lo mio secreto non era comunicato lo giorno altrui per mia vista. E mantenente pensai di fare di questa gentile donna schermo de la veritade; e tanto ne mostrai in poco tempo, che lo mio secreto fue creduto sapere da le più persone che di me ragionavano. Con questa donna mi celai alquanti anni e mesi; e per più fare credente altrui, feci per lei certe cosette per rima, le quali non è mio intendimento di scrivere qui, se non in quanto facesse a trattare di quella gentilissima Beatrice; e però le lascerò tutte, salvo che alcuna cosa ne scriverò che pare che sia loda di lei.

VI. Dico che in questo tempo che questa donna era schermo di tanto amore, quanto da la mia parte, sì mi venne una volontade di volere ricordare lo nome di quella gentilissima ed accompagnarlo di molti nomi di donne, e spezialmente del nome di questa gentile

saw all the worth." And that was nearly the beginning of the friend-
ship between us, when he learned that it was I who had sent him that.
The true meaning of the aforesaid dream was not seen by anyone at
that time, but now it is perfectly obvious even to the most naive.

IV. From that vision on, my natural spirit began to be hindered in its
functions, because my soul was fully occupied by thoughts of that most
noble lady; so that shortly afterward I became so frail and weak in body
that the sight of me grieved many friends; and many people who were
filled with envy were already striving to learn about me that which I
wanted to conceal from others completely. And I, aware of the ill-
intentioned questions they asked of me, would reply, by the will of Love,
who was directing me according to the advice of reason, that it was Love
who had ruled me in that manner. I admitted it was Love because I bore
so many of his signs on my face that this could not be concealed. And
when they asked me, "For whose sake has this Love so undone you?," I
would look at them with a smile, but would tell them nothing.

V. It befell one day that that most noble lady was seated where
words praising the Queen of Glory were being chanted, and I was po-
sitioned where I could behold my bliss; in a straight line between us
sat a very good-looking gentlewoman, who gazed at me frequently,
surprised at my staring, which seemed to be directed at *her*. Where-
upon many people noticed her gaze; and so much attention was paid
to it that, as I left that place, I heard someone behind me saying: "See
how that lady is destroying that man's constitution!" When she was
mentioned by name, I realized that the speaker meant the woman
who had been seated at the center of the straight line originating at
the most noble Beatrice and ending at my eyes. Then I was greatly
comforted, assuring myself that my secret had not been divulged to
others that day by my glances. And at once I hit on the idea of mak-
ing that gentlewoman a screen to hide the truth; and before long I
made so many demonstrations of affection that most of the people
who discussed me thought they knew my secret. I concealed myself
by means of that woman for several years and months; and to make
others believe this more firmly, I dedicated certain little poems to her,
which it is not my intention to set down here, except to the extent that
they involve that most noble Beatrice; and so I shall omit them all, but
I shall make some mention of them which seems to be in praise of her.

VI. To continue: in that period when that woman was the screen
concealing the great love I for my part was experiencing, I felt the de-
sire to set down the name of that most noble lady Beatrice, accompa-
nying it by many other women's names, especially the name of the

donna. E presi li nomi di sessanta le più belle donne de la cittade ove
la mia donna fue posta da l'altissimo sire, e compuosi una pistola sotto
forma di serventese, la quale io non scriverò: e non n'avrei fatto men-
zione, se non per dire quello che, componendola, maravigliosamente
addivenne, cioè che in alcuno altro numero non sofferse lo nome de
la mia donna stare, se non in su lo nove, tra li nomi di queste donne.

VII. La donna co la quale io avea tanto tempo celata la mia volon-
tade, convenne che si partisse de la sopradetta cittade e andasse in
paese molto lontano; per che io, quasi sbigottito de la bella difesa che
m'era venuta meno, assai me ne disconfortai, più che io medesimo
non avrei creduto dinanzi. E pensando che se de la sua partita io non
parlasse alquanto dolorosamente, le persone sarebbero accorte più
tosto de lo mio nascondere, propuosi di farne alcuna lamentanza in
uno sonetto; lo quale io scriverò, acciò che la mia donna fue imme-
diata cagione di certe parole che ne lo sonetto sono, sì come appare a
chi lo intende. E allora dissi questo sonetto, che comincia: *O voi che
per la via.*

> O voi che per la via d'Amor passate,
>   attendete e guardate
>   s'elli è dolore alcun, quanto 'l mio, grave;
>   e prego sol ch'audir mi sofferiate,
>   e poi imaginate
>   s'io son d'ogni tormento ostale e chiave.
>   Amor, non già per mia poca bontate,
>   ma per sua nobiltate,
>   mi pose in vita sì dolce e soave,
>   ch'io mi sentia dir dietro spesse fiate:
>   «Deo, per qual dignitate
>   così leggiadro questi lo core have?»
> Or ho perduta tutta mia baldanza,
>   che si movea d'amoroso tesoro;
>   ond'io pover dimoro,
>   in guisa che di dir mi ven dottanza.
>   Sì che volendo far come coloro
>   che per vergogna celan lor mancanza,
>   di fuor mostro allegranza,
>   e dentro da lo core struggo e ploro.

gentlewoman my name was linked with. And I took the names of the sixty most beautiful women in the city where the Lord on high had placed my lady, and I composed an epistle in the form of a *sirventes*,[10] which I shall not copy here; I would not have mentioned it, except to state something remarkable that occurred as I composed it: among the names of those women, that of my lady refused to be listed in any other place than ninth.

VII. The woman through whom I had concealed my true leanings for so long had to leave the aforesaid city and journey to a very distant land; so that I, nearly dismayed at the loss of my fine smokescreen, was greatly dispirited, more than I myself would have believed previously. And thinking that, if I failed to make some sorrowful mention of her departure, people would more readily become aware of my subterfuge, I resolved to lament it somewhat in a sonnet, which I shall set down because my lady was the immediate inspiration for certain passages in the sonnet, as will be evident to careful readers. And then I wrote this sonnet,[11] which begins "O you who walk along."

> O you who walk along the path of Love,
>   look and see
>   whether there is any sorrow as grievous as mine;
>   and I ask only that you allow me to be heard,
>   and then judge
>   whether I am not the hostel and key of every torment.
>   Love, not for the slight goodness in me,
>   but through his own nobility,
>   placed me in a life so sweet and gentle
>   that I often heard people behind me say:
>   "God, in return for what worth
>   does this fellow have such a cheerful heart?"
> Now I have lost all my self-assurance,
>   which arose from possessing a treasure of love;
>   so that I remain impoverished,
>   in such manner that I hesitate to state it.
>   And so, wishing to imitate those
>   who conceal their want out of shame,
>   I display a merry exterior,
>   but in my heart I am consumed and I lament.

---

10. A type of Provençal poem, often satirical.   11. This sonnet, like another that follows, is a double, or doubled, sonnet, in which shorter lines (in the basic rhyme scheme) are inserted among the fourteen long lines.

Questo sonetto ha due parti principali; che ne la prima intendo chiamare li fedeli d'Amore per quelle parole di Geremia profeta che dicono: «O vos omnes qui transitis per viam, attendite et videte si est dolor sicut dolor meus», e pregare che mi sofferino d'audire; ne la seconda narro là ove Amore m'avea posto, con altro intendimento che l'estreme parti del sonetto non mostrano, e dico che io hoe ciò perduto. La seconda parte comincia quivi: *Amor, non già.*

VIII. Appresso lo partire di questa gentile donna fue piacere del segnore de li angeli di chiamare a la sua gloria una donna giovane e di gentile aspetto molto, la quale fue assai graziosa in questa sopradetta cittade; lo cui corpo io vidi giacere sanza l'anima in mezzo di molte donne, le quali piangeano assai pietosamente. Allora, ricordandomi che già l'avea veduta fare compagnia a quella gentilissima, non poteo sostenere alquante lagrime; anzi piangendo mi propuosi di dicere alquante parole de la sua morte, in guiderdone di ciò che alcuna fiata l'avea veduta con la mia donna. E di ciò toccai alcuna cosa ne l'ultima parte de le parole che io ne dissi, sì come appare manifestamente a chi lo intende. E dissi allora questi due sonetti, li quali comincia lo primo: *Piangete, amanti,* e lo secondo: *Morte villana.*

> Piangete, amanti, poi che piange Amore,
>   udendo qual cagion lui fa plorare.
>   Amor sente a Pietà donne chiamare,
>   mostrando amaro duol per li occhi fore,
>   perchè villana Morte in gentil core
>   ha miso il suo crudele adoperare,
>   guastando ciò che al mondo è da laudare
>   in gentil donna sovra de l'onore.
> Audite quanto Amor le fece orranza,
>   ch'io 'l vidi lamentare in forma vera
>   sovra la morta imagine avvenente;
>   e riguardava ver lo ciel sovente,
>   ove l'alma gentil già locata era,
>   che donna fu di sì gaia sembianza.

Questo primo sonetto si divide in tre parti: ne la prima chiamo e sollicito li fedeli d'Amore a piangere e dico che lo segnore loro piange, e dico —udendo la cagione per che piange,— acciò che s'acconcino più ad ascoltarmi; ne la seconda narro la cagione; ne la terza parlo d'al-

This sonnet has two main parts; in the first, my intention is to summon the devotees of Love in the words of the prophet Jeremiah,[12] "All ye that pass by . . . behold, and see if there be any sorrow like unto my sorrow," and beg them to deign to hear me; in the second, I tell where Love had placed me, in a position so different from that at the end of the sonnet, and I state that I have lost this. The second part begins with the words "Love, not for the slight goodness."

VIII. After the departure of that gentlewoman it pleased the Lord of the angels to call to his glory a young woman of very pleasing appearance who had been a very charming inhabitant of the aforesaid city; I saw her body lying lifeless amid many women who were lamenting her most compassionately. Then, recalling that I had formerly seen her in the company of that most noble lady, I was unable to hold back a few tears; in fact, as I wept I resolved to write a poem concerning her death, in recompense for having seen her at times with my lady. And I alluded slightly to this in the last part of the poem I wrote, as will be evident to careful readers. And I then wrote these two sonnets, one beginning "Weep, lovers," and the other, "Cruel Death."

> Weep, lovers, since Love is weeping,
>   as you hear the cause of his lament.
>   Love hears women crying "Pity,"
>   showing bitter grief in their eyes,
>   because cruel Death has laid
>   its rough hands on a gentle heart,
>   spoiling that which is most to be praised in the world
>   in a gentlewoman, save honor.
> Hear what respect Love paid to her,
>   for I saw him lamenting in genuine fashion
>   over the charming dead image;
>   and he frequently looked heavenward,
>   where the noble soul was already located,
>   she who had been a woman of such cheerful aspect.

This first sonnet is divided into three parts: in the first, I summon and arouse the devotees of Love to weep, saying that their master is weeping, and I say "as you hear the cause of his lament" so they will prepare themselves better to hear me out; in the second, I tell the

---

12. Lamentations 1:12.

cuno onore che Amore fece a questa donna. La seconda parte comincia quivi: *Amor sente;* la terza quivi: *Audite.*

> Morte villana, di pietà nemica,
>   di dolor madre antica,
>   giudicio incontastabile gravoso,
>   poi che hai data matera al cor doglioso
>   ond'io vado pensoso,
>   di te blasmar la lingua s'affatica.
> E s'io di grazia ti voi far mendica,
>   convenesi ch'eo dica
>   lo tuo fallar d'onni torto tortoso,
>   non però ch'a la gente sia nascoso,
>   ma per farne cruccioso
>   chi d'amor per innanzi si notrica.
> Dal secolo hai partita cortesia
>   e ciò ch'è in donna da pregiar vertute:
>   in gaia gioventute
>   distrutta hai l'amorosa leggiadria.
>   Più non voi discovrir qual donna sia
>   che per le propietà sue canosciute.
>   Chi non merta salute
>   non speri mai d'aver sua compagnia.

Questo sonetto si divide in quattro parti: ne la prima parte chiamo la Morte per certi suoi nomi propri; ne la seconda, parlando a lei, dico la cagione per che io mi muovo a blasimarla; ne la terza la vitupero; ne la quarta mi volgo a parlare a indiffinita persona, avvegna che quanto a lo mio intendimento sia diffinita. La seconda comincia quivi: *poi che hai data;* la terza quivi: *E s'io di grazia;* la quarta quivi: *Chi non merta salute.*

IX. Appresso la morte di questa donna alquanti die avvenne cosa per la quale me convenne partire de la sopradetta cittade e ire verso quelle parti dov'era la gentile donna ch'era stata mia difesa, avvegna che non tanto fosse lontano lo termine de lo mio andare quanto ella era. E tutto ch'io fosse a la compagnia di molti quanto a la vista, l'andare mi dispiacea sì, che quasi li sospiri non poteano disfogare l'angoscia che lo cuore sentia, però ch'io mi dilungava de la mia beatitudine. E però lo dolcissimo segnore, lo quale mi segnoreggiava per la vertù de la gentilissima donna, ne la mia imaginazione apparve come peregrino leggeramente vestito e di vili drappi. Elli mi parea disbigottito, e guardava la terra, salvo che talora li suoi occhi mi parea che

cause; in the third, I speak of some respect that Love paid that lady. The second part begins with "Love hears"; the third, with "Hear."

> Cruel Death, enemy to pity,
>   ancient mother of sorrow,
>   burdensome, ineluctable sentencer,
>   since you have supplied matter to my grieving heart,
>   so that I go about pensively,
>   my tongue tires itself out reproaching you.
>   And if I want to make you beg for mercy,
>   I need only mention
>   your crime, guilty of every wrong,
>   so that it may not be concealed from people;
>   rather, to make those angry at it
>   who will be nurtured by love in the future.
> From this world you have severed courtesy
>   and that which it is virtuous to praise in woman:
>   in cheerful youth
>   you have destroyed loving charm.
>   I wish to reveal no further which woman this is
>   except by her well-known characteristics.
>   Let those who do not merit salvation
>   never hope to enjoy her company.

This sonnet is divided into four parts: in the first, I call Death by certain names appropriate to it; in the second, addressing Death, I state my reason for reproaching it; in the third, I revile it; in the fourth, I turn to address an unspecified person, though I have a specific one in mind. The second part begins with "since you have supplied"; the third, with "And if I want"; the fourth, with "Let those who do not merit."

IX. A few days after the death of that lady, something occurred that made me leave the aforesaid city in the direction of the place where my smokescreen gentlewoman was residing, although the goal of my journey was not as distant as that place. And, despite the fact that, seemingly, I had a lot of company, the departure irked me so much that my sighs were all but unable to relieve the anguish I felt in my heart on leaving my bliss far behind. And so my most sweet master, who ruled me through the power of that most noble lady, appeared in my imaginings in the form of a pilgrim scantily clad in cheap clothing. He seemed to me to be dismayed, looking down at the ground except for some moments when I thought his eyes turned toward a beautiful,

si volgessero ad uno fiume bello e corrente e chiarissimo, lo quale sen
gia lungo questo cammino là ov'io era. A me parve che Amore mi chia-
masse, e dicessemi queste parole: «Io vegno da quella donna la quale
è stata tua lunga difesa, e so che lo suo rivenire non sarà a gran tempi;
e però quello cuore che io ti facea avere a lei, io l'ho meco, e portolo
a donna la quale sarà tua difensione, come questa era». E nominollami
per nome, sì che io la conobbi bene. «Ma tuttavia, di queste parole
ch'io t'ho ragionate se alcuna cosa ne dicessi, dille nel modo che per
loro non si discernesse lo simulato amore che tu hai mostrato a questa
e che ti converrà mostrare ad altri». E dette queste parole, disparve
questa mia imaginazione tutta subitamente per la grandissima parte
che mi parve che Amore mi desse di sè; e, quasi cambiato ne la vista
mia, cavalcai quel giorno pensoso molto e accompagnato da molti
sospiri. Appresso lo giorno cominciai di ciò questo sonetto, lo quale
comincia: *Cavalcando*.

> Cavalcando l'altr'ier per un cammino,
>   pensoso de l'andar che mi sgradia,
>   trovai Amore in mezzo de la via
>   in abito leggier di peregrino.
>   Ne la sembianza mi parea meschino,
>   come avesse perduto segnoria;
>   e sospirando pensoso venia,
>   per non veder la gente, a capo chino.
> Quando mi vide, mi chiamò per nome,
>   e disse: «Io vegno di lontana parte,
>   ov'era lo tuo cor per mio volere;
>   e recolo a servir novo piacere».
>   Allora presi di lui sì gran parte,
>   ch'elli disparve, e non m'accorsi come.

Questo sonetto ha tre parti: ne la prima parte dico sì com'io trovai
Amore, e quale mi parea; ne la seconda dico quello ch'elli mi disse,
avvegna che non compiutamente per tema ch'avea di discovrire lo mio
secreto; ne la terza dico com'elli mi disparve. La seconda comincia
quivi: *Quando mi vide;* la terza: *Allora presi.*

X. Appresso la mia ritornata mi misi a cercare di questa donna che
lo mio segnore m'avea nominata ne lo cammino de li sospiri; e acciò
che lo mio parlare sia più brieve, dico che in poco tempo la feci mia
difesa tanto, che troppa gente ne ragionava oltre li termini de la corte-
sia; onde molte fiate mi pensava duramente. E per questa cagione,
cioè di questa soverchievole voce che parea che m'infamasse viziosa-

flowing, very clear river, which ran alongside the road I was on. I thought that he, Love, was calling me, speaking these words: "I have come from that woman who has long been your screen, and I know that she will not return for a long time yet; therefore that heart of yours which I had held in keeping for her I now have with me, and I am transferring it to another woman who will be a shield to you as she was." And he named her to me, so that I was well aware who she was. "But nevertheless, if you reveal anything of these words I have spoken to you, do so in such a way that no one will thereby discern the feigned love you showed to that woman and which you will need to show to this new one." And, after those words were spoken, this vision of mine suddenly vanished completely because of Love's seemingly very great embodiment in me; and, all but transformed in appearance, I rode that day lost in thought and accompanied by many sighs. The following day I began writing this sonnet about it, which begins "Riding."

> Riding along a road the other day,
>> brooding over the journey, which displeased me,
>> I found Love in the middle of the road
>> in the scanty garb of a pilgrim.
>> He seemed to me wretched in appearance,
>> as if he had lost his dominion;
>> and he walked along sighing pensively,
>> his head lowered, to avoid looking at people.
> When he saw me, he called me by name,
>> saying: "I have come from distant parts,
>> where your heart was located at my wishes;
>> and I am returning it to serve my new pleasure."
>> Then I partook of so great a share of him
>> that he vanished, and I did not notice how.

This sonnet has three parts: in the first part I tell how I found Love, and how he seemed to me; in the second, I tell what he said to me, though not completely, because I feared I might reveal my secret; in the third, I tell how he vanished from my sight. The second part begins with "When he saw me"; the third, with "Then I partook."

X. After my return I began to seek out that woman whom my master had named to me on the road of sighs; and, to abridge my narrative, I say that before long I made her into so much of a screen that too many people were discussing it beyond the limits of politeness; so that I often had harsh thoughts about this. And for that reason—that is, because of the excessive hue and cry that seemed to be making me

mente, quella gentilissima, la quale fue distruggitrice di tutti li vizi e
regina de le virtudi, passando per alcuna parte, mi negò lo suo dolcis-
simo salutare, ne lo quale stava tutta la mia beatitudine. E uscendo
alquanto del proposito presente, voglio dare a intendere quello che lo
suo salutare in me vertuosamente operava.

XI. Dico che quando ella apparia da parte alcuna, per la speranza
de la mirabile salute nullo nemico mi rimanea, anzi mi giugnea una
fiamma di caritate, la quale mi facea perdonare a chiunque m'avesse
offeso; e chi allora m'avesse domandato di cosa alcuna, la mia rispon-
sione sarebbe stata solamente —Amore,— con viso vestito d'umili-
tade. E quando ella fosse alquanto propinqua al salutare, uno spirito
d'amore, distruggendo tutti li altri spiriti sensitivi, pingea fuori li de-
boletti spiriti del viso, e dicea loro: «Andate a onorare la donna vo-
stra»; ed elli si rimanea nel luogo loro. E chi avesse voluto conoscere
Amore, fare lo potea mirando lo tremare de li occhi miei. E quando
questa gentilissima salute salutava, non che Amore fosse tal mezzo
che potesse obumbrare a me la intollerabile beatitudine, ma elli quasi
per soverchio di dolcezza divenia tale, che lo mio corpo, lo quale era
tutto allora sotto lo suo reggimento, molte volte si movea come cosa
grave inanimata. Sì che appare manifestamente che ne le sue salute
abitava la mia beatitudine, la quale molte volte passava e redundava la
mia capacitade.

XII. Ora, tornando al proposito, dico che poi che la mia beatitudine
mi fue negata, mi giunse tanto dolore, che, partito me da le genti, in
solinga parte andai a bagnare la terra d'amarissime lagrime. E poi che
alquanto mi fue sollenato questo lagrimare, misimi ne la mia camera,
là ov'io potea lamentarmi sanza essere udito; e quivi, chiamando mi-
sericordia a la donna de la cortesia, e dicendo «Amore, aiuta lo tuo
fedele», m'addormentai come un pargoletto battuto lagrimando.
Avvenne quasi nel mezzo de lo mio dormire che me parve vedere ne
la mia camera lungo me sedere uno giovane vestito di bianchissime
vestimenta, e pensando molto quanto a la vista sua, mi riguardava là
ov'io giacea; e quando m'avea guardato alquanto, pareami che sospi-
rando mi chiamasse, e diceami queste parole: «Fili mi, tempus est ut
pretermictantur simulacra nostra». Allora mi parea che io lo
conoscesse, però che mi chiamava così come assai fiate ne li miei
sonni m'avea già chiamato: e riguardandolo, parvemi che piangesse
pietosamente, e parea che attendesse da me alcuna parola; ond'io, as-
sicurandomi, cominciai a parlare così con esso: «Segnore de la nobil-
tade, e perchè piangi tu?». E quelli mi dicea queste parole: «Ego tan-
quam centrum circuli, cui simili modo se habent circumferentie

infamous for vice—when that most noble lady, who was the destroyer of every vice and the queen of virtues, was walking in some place, she denied me her most sweet greeting, in which all my bliss consisted. And, digressing a little from the present topic, I wish to make it understood what her greeting brought about in me by its virtuous power.

XI. Whenever she appeared anywhere, in my expectation of that wondrous salutary greeting, I had no enemies left; on the contrary, I was overcome by a flame of charitable feeling, which made me forgive whoever had offended me; and if anyone had asked me for anything at such times, my reply would have been merely "Love," with my face garbed in humility. And whenever she was nearly about to greet me, a spirit of love, destroying all other sensory spirits, drove out the feeble spirits of my eyes, telling them, "Go and honor your lady," and it would take their place. And anyone who wanted to recognize Love could have done so by looking at the trembling of my eyes. And whenever she extended that most noble greeting, not only was Love no intermediary who might diminish my unbearable bliss, but by a surfeit of sweetness he became such that my body, completely under his control at such times, often moved like a heavy, lifeless mass. So that it is clearly evident that my bliss consisted in her greetings, a bliss that often surpassed and went beyond my capacities.

XII. Now, returning to the subject, I continue. After my bliss was denied me, I felt such grief that I withdrew from company and went to some lonely spot to bathe the ground with most bitter tears. And after that weeping of mine had calmed down a little, I shut myself up in my room, where I could lament without being heard; and there, calling for mercy from the lady of courtesy and saying, "Love, aid your devotee," I fell asleep in tears like a little boy who had been beaten. Nearly halfway through my slumber it came about that I thought I saw seated beside me in my room a young man clad in very white garments, who, seemingly lost in thought, looked at me as I lay there; and after looking at me a while, he called to me with a sigh, as I thought, and spoke these words to me: "My son, it is time for our feigning to be put aside." Then it seemed to me that I knew him, because he called to me in the way he had called me very often in the past during my slumbers: as I looked at him again, I thought he was weeping compassionately, and he appeared to be awaiting some word from me; so that, taking heart, I began to address him thus: "Lord of nobility, why do you weep?" And he answered me as follows: "I am like the fixed center of a circle, from which all points of the circumference are equidistant; but you are not firm like that." Then, pondering his words, I felt that he had spoken to me very

partes; tu autem non sic». Allora, pensando a le sue parole, mi parea
che m'avesse parlato molto oscuramente; sì ch'io mi sforzava di par-
lare, e diceali queste parole: «Che è ciò, segnore, che mi parli con
tanta oscuritade?». E quelli mi dicea in parole volgari: «Non diman-
dare più che utile ti sia». E però cominciai allora con lui a ragionare
de la salute la quale mi fue negata, e domandailo de la cagione; onde
in questa guisa da lui mi fue risposto: «Quella nostra Beatrice udio da
certe persone di te ragionando, che la donna la quale io ti nominai nel
cammino de li sospiri, ricevea da te alcuna noia; e però questa gen-
tilissima, la quale è contraria di tutte le noie, non degnò salutare la tua
persona, temendo non fosse noiosa. Onde con ciò sia cosa che vera-
cemente sia conosciuto per lei alquanto lo tuo secreto per lunga con-
suetudine, voglio che tu dichi certe parole per rima, ne le quali tu
comprendi la forza che io tegno sopra te per lei, e come tu fosti suo
tostamente da la tua puerizia. E di ciò chiama testimonio colui che lo
sa, e come tu prieghi lui che li le dica; ed io, che son quelli, volentieri
le ne ragionerò; e per questo sentirà ella la tua volontade, la quale sen-
tendo, conoscerà le parole de li ingannati. Queste parole fa che siano
quasi un mezzo, sì che tu non parli a lei immediatamente, che non è
degno; e no le mandare in parte, sanza me, ove potessero essere in-
tese da lei, ma falle adornare di soave armonia, ne la quale io sarò
tutte le volte che farà mestiere». E dette queste parole, sì disparve, e
lo mio sonno fue rotto. Onde io ricordandomi, trovai che questa vi-
sione m'era apparita ne la nona ora del die; e anzi ch'io uscisse di
questa camera, propuosi di fare una ballata, ne la quale io seguitasse
ciò che lo mio segnore m'avea imposto; e feci poi questa ballata, che
comincia: *Ballata, i'voi.*

> Ballata, i'voi che tu ritrovi Amore,
>   e con lui vade a madonna davante,
>   sì che la scusa mia, la qual tu cante,
>   ragioni poi con lei lo mio segnore.
> Tu vai, ballata, sì cortesemente,
>   che sanza compagnia
>   dovresti avere in tutte parti ardire;
>   ma se tu vuoli andar sicuramente,
>   retrova l'Amor pria,
>   chè forse non è bon sanza lui gire;
>   però che quella che ti dee audire,
>   sì com'io credo, è ver di me adirata:
>   se tu di lui non fossi accompagnata,

obscurely; so that I made an effort to speak, and I addressed him in these words: "Master, what is this that you tell me so obscurely?" And he said, speaking in the vernacular: "Do not ask for more than is useful to you." And so I then began to talk to him about the salutary greeting that had been denied me, and I asked him the reason; the reply to which was in this manner: "That Beatrice of ours heard from certain persons discussing you that the lady I named to you on the road of sighs was receiving some vexation from you; and so that most noble lady, who is an enemy to all vexation, did not deign to greet you, fearing lest she cause vexation. Therefore, inasmuch as your secret is truly known to her in part, because of her long experience of you, I want you to write a poem in which you acknowledge the power I wield over you through her, and in which you say you were hers at once and have been ever since you were a boy. And summon as a witness to that the one who knows it, and say that you beg him to tell her so; and I, who am that witness, will gladly speak to her about it; and thereby she will perceive your wishes and, perceiving them, she will take at their true value the reports of the people you have fooled. Write the poem in such a way that those words will be an intermediary, so to speak, so that you are not addressing her directly, which would be improper; and do not send the poem, without me, anywhere that it could be heard by her, but have it set to sweet music, in which I shall be found every time that it is necessary." And having spoken those words, he vanished, and my slumber was broken. Remembering this, I found that that vision had appeared to me in the ninth hour of the day; and before I left that room, I decided to write a poem in *ballata* form, in which I would obey my master's commands; and then I wrote this *ballata*, which begins "*Ballata*, I want you."

> *Ballata*, I want you to seek out Love,
>> and go with him to where my lady is,
>> so that my apology, which you are to sing,
>> my master can then discuss with her.
> You go, *ballata*, so courteously
>> that, even without company,
>> you ought to be confident anywhere;
>> but if you wish to go securely,
>> seek out Love first,
>> for perhaps it is not good to go without him;
>> because the lady who is to hear you,
>> as I believe, is angry with me:
>> if you were not accompanied by him,

leggeramente ti faria disnore.
Con dolze sono, quando se' con lui,
   comincia este parole,
   appresso che averai chesta pietate:
   «Madonna, quelli che mi manda a vui,
   quando vi piaccia, vole,
   sed elli ha scusa, che la m'intendiate.
   Amore è qui, che per vostra bieltate
   lo face, come vol, vista cangiare:
   dunque perchè li fece altra guardare
   pensatel voi, da che non mutò 'l core.»
Dille: «Madonna, lo suo core è stato
   con sì fermàta fede,
   che 'n voi servir l'ha 'mpronto onne pensero:
   tosto fu vostro, e mai non s'è smagato».
   Sed ella non ti crede,
   dì che domandi Amor, che sa lo vero:
   ed a la fine falle umil preghero,
   lo perdonare se le fosse a noia,
   che mi comandi per messo ch'eo moia,
   e vedrassi ubidir ben servidore.
E dì a colui ch'è d'ogni pietà chiave,
   avante che sdonnei,
   che le saprà contar mia ragion bona:
   «Per grazia de la mia nota soave
   reman tu qui con lei,
   e del tuo servo ciò che vuoi ragiona;
   e s'ella per tuo prego li perdona,
   fa che li annunzi un bel sembiante pace».
   Gentil ballata mia, quando ti piace,
   movi in quel punto che tu n'aggie onore.

Questa ballata in tre parti si divide: ne la prima dico a lei ov'ella vada, e confortola però che vada più sicura, e dico ne la cui compagnia si metta, se vuole sicuramente andare e sanza pericolo alcuno; ne la seconda dico quello che lei si pertiene di fare intendere; ne la terza la licenzio del gire quando vuole, raccomandando lo suo movimento ne le braccia de la fortuna. La seconda parte comincia quivi: *Con dolze sono;* la terza quivi: *Gentil ballata.*

Potrebbe già l'uomo opporre contra me e dicere che non sapesse a cui fosse lo mio parlare in seconda persona, però che la ballata non è altro che queste parole ched io parlo: e però dico che questo dubbio

she would easily show you disrespect.
With sweet music, once you are with him,
   begin these words,
   after you have asked for pity:
   "My lady, the man who sends me to you,
   may it please you, wishes,
   if he has an apology, that you hear me state it.
   Love is here, who through your beauty
   makes him turn pale at will:
   therefore, consider well why he made him
   look at another woman, since his heart has not changed."
Tell her: "My lady, his heart has remained
   so firmly faithful
   that his whole mind is set on serving you:
   he was yours at once, and has never strayed."
   If she does not believe you,
   tell her to ask Love, who knows the truth:
   and finally beg her humbly,
   in case it vexes her to forgive me,
   to order me, by messenger, to die
   and she will see her loyal servant obey.
And tell him who is the key to all compassion,
   before you leave off serving my lady,
   for he will be able to convey my good thoughts:
   "Through the charm of my gentle notes
   remain here with her,
   and say whatever you like about your slave;
   and if she forgives him at your request,
   have her kindly face proclaim peace to him."
   My noble *ballata*, whenever you like,
   go to that place where you will gain honor.

This *ballata* is divided into three parts: in the first, I tell it where to go, and encourage it so that it will go with greater confidence, and I tell it whose company to seek, if it wishes to go safely and without any danger; in the second, I tell it what it pertains to it to communicate; in the third, I give it leave to go whenever it likes, commending its journey to the arms of Fortune. The second part begins with the words "With sweet music"; the third, with "My noble *ballata*."

Someone might criticize me, saying he does not know whom I am addressing in the second person, because the *ballata* is identical with the words I am uttering: therefore I say that I intend to dispel that

io lo intendo solvere e dichiarare in questo libello ancora in parte più
dubbiosa; e allora intenda qui chi qui dubita, o chi qui volesse opporre
in questo modo.

XIII. Appresso di questa soprascritta visione, avendo già dette le
parole che Amore m'avea imposte a dire, mi cominciaro molti e di-
versi pensamenti a combattere e a tentare, ciascuno quasi indefensi-
bilemente; tra li quali pensamenti quattro mi parea che ingom-
brassero più lo riposo de la vita. L'uno de i quali era questo: buona è
la signoria d'Amore, però che trae lo intendimento del suo fedele da
tutte le vili cose. L'altro era questo: non buona è la signoria d'Amore,
però che quanto lo suo fedele più fede li porta, tanto più gravi e do-
lorosi punti li conviene passare. L'altro era questo: lo nome d'Amore
è sì dolce a udire, che impossibile mi pare che la sua propria opera-
zione sia ne le più cose altro che dolce, con ciò sia cosa che li nomi se-
guitino le nominate cose, sì come è scritto: «Nomina sunt consequen-
tia rerum». Lo quarto era questo: la donna per cui Amore ti stringe
così, non è come l'altre donne, che leggeramente si muova del suo
cuore. E ciascuno mi combattea tanto, che mi facea stare quasi come
colui che non sa per qual via pigli lo suo cammino, e che vuole andare
e non sa onde se ne vada; e se io pensava di volere cercare una co-
mune via di costoro, cioè là ove tutti s'accordassero, questa era via
molto inimica verso me, cioè di chiamare e di mettermi ne le braccia
de la Pietà. E in questo stato dimorando, mi giunse volontade di
scriverne parole rimate; e dissine allora questo sonetto, lo quale co-
mincia: *Tutti li miei penser.*

> Tutti li miei penser parlan d'Amore;
>   e hanno in lor sì gran varietate,
>   ch'altro mi fa voler sua potestate,
>   altro folle ragiona il suo valore,
>   altro sperando m'apporta dolzore,
>   altro pianger mi fa spesse fiate;
>   e sol s'accordano in cherer pietate,
>   tremando di paura che è nel core.
> Ond'io non so da qual matera prenda;
>   e vorrei dire, e non so ch'io mi dica:
>   così mi trovo in amorosa erranza!
>   E se con tutti voi fare accordanza,
>   convenemi chiamar la mia nemica,
>   madonna la Pietà, che mi difenda.

doubt and explain this later in an even more difficult part of this little book; at that time, let that man who has doubts here, or wishes to criticize me here in this way, understand this passage.

XIII. After the aforesaid vision, when I had already spoken the words Love had ordered me to speak, many different thoughts began to assail and try me, each of them almost irresistibly; among those thoughts, four seemed to encumber most my peace of mind. One of them was this: Love's domination is good, because it distracts his devotee's mind from everything that is base. The second was this: Love's domination is not good, because the more loyal his follower is to him, the more burdensome and sorrowful experiences he must undergo. The third was this: the name of Love is so sweet to the ear that I feel it impossible for his personal actions to be other than sweet in most cases, inasmuch as names are in accordance with the things they name, as it is written: "Names are the consequences of the things."[13] The fourth was this: the lady on whose account Love is binding you this way is not like other women, one who will easily change her affections. And each of these thoughts assailed me so violently that it nearly made me act like a man who does not know which path to take on his journey, a man who wishes to proceed but does not know in which direction; and whenever I thought of trying to find a path common to them all—that is, one which would bring them all into agreement—it was a path very hostile to me: the path of calling for, and placing myself in the arms of, Pity. And remaining in that condition, I felt the desire to write a poem about it; and I then wrote this sonnet, which begins "All my thoughts."

> All my thoughts speak of Love;
>   but they differ so much among themselves
>   that one of them makes me wish for his power,
>   another declares his domination to be mad,
>   another brings me sweetness by way of hope,
>   another makes me frequently weep;
>   they only agree in asking for pity,
>   trembling with the fear that is in my heart.
> So that I do not know which material to use;
>   and I want to speak, but do not know what to say:
>   so great is my confusion in love!
>   And if I want to bring them all into accord,
>   I must call upon my enemy,
>   lady Pity, to protect me.

13. A tenet of Roman law and medieval scholasticism.

Questo sonetto in quattro parti si può dividere: ne la prima dico e soppongo che tutti li miei pensieri sono d'Amore; ne la seconda dico che sono diversi, e narro la loro diversitade; ne la terza dico in che tutti pare che s'accordino; ne la quarta dico che volendo dire d'Amore, non so da qual parte pigli matera, e se la voglio pigliare da tutti, convene che io chiami la mia inimica, madonna la Pietade; e dico — madonna— quasi per disdegnoso modo di parlare. La seconda parte comincia quivi: *e hanno in lor;* la terza quivi: *e sol s'accordano;* la quarta quivi: *Ond'io non so.*

XIV. Appresso la battaglia de li diversi pensieri avvenne che questa gentilissima venne in parte ove molte donne gentili erano adunate; a la qual parte io fui condotto per amica persona, credendosi fare a me grande piacere, in quanto mi menava là ove tante donne mostravano le loro bellezze. Onde io, quasi no sappiendo a che io fossi menato, e fidandomi ne la persona la quale uno suo amico a l'estremitade de la vita condotto avea, dissi a lui: «Perchè semo noi venuti a queste donne?». Allora quelli mi disse: «Per fare sì ch'elle siano degnamente servite». E lo vero è che adunate quivi erano a la compagnia d'una gentile donna che disposata era lo giorno; e però, secondo l'usanza de la sopradetta cittade, convenia che le facessero compagnia nel primo sedere a la mensa che facea ne la magione del suo novello sposo. Sì che io, credendomi fare piacere di questo amico, propuosi di stare al servigio de le donne ne la sua compagnia. E nel fine del mio proponimento mi parve sentire uno mirabile tremore incominciare nel mio petto da la sinistra parte e distendersi di subito per tutte le parti del mio corpo. Allora dico che io poggiai la mia persona simulatamente ad una pintura la quale circundava questa magione; e temendo non altri si fosse accorto del mio tremare, levai li occhi, e mirando le donne, vidi tra loro la gentilissima Beatrice. Allora fuoro sì distrutti li miei spiriti per la forza che Amore prese veggendosi in tanta propinquitade a la gentilissima donna, che non ne rimasero in vita più che li spiriti del viso; e ancora questi rimasero fuori de li loro istrumenti, però che Amore volea stare nel loro nobilissimo luogo per vedere la mirabile donna. E avvegna che io fossi altro che prima, molto mi dolea di questi spiritelli, che si lamentavano forte e diceano: «Se questi non ci infolgorasse così fuori del nostro luogo, noi potremmo stare a vedere la maraviglia di questa donna così come stanno li altri nostri pari». Io dico che molte di queste donne, accorgendosi de la mia trasfigurazione, si cominciaro a maravigliare, e ragionando si gabbavano di me con questa gentilissima; onde lo ingannato amico di buona fede mi prese per la mano, e traendomi fuori de la veduta di queste donne, sì

This sonnet can be divided into four parts: in the first, I state and declare that all my thoughts are of Love; in the second, I say that they differ and I tell how they differ; in the third, I say in what way they all seem to agree; in the fourth, I say that, wishing to speak of Love, I do not know where to obtain my material, and if I want to obtain it from all the thoughts, I must call upon my enemy, lady Pity; and I call her my lady in a more or less scornful manner of speaking. The second part begins with the words "but they differ"; the third, with "they only agree"; the fourth, with "So that I do not know."

XIV. After that combat with the conflicting thoughts, it befell that that most noble lady came to a place where many gentlewomen were assembled; to that place I was brought by a friendly person who thought he would give me great pleasure by taking me where so many women displayed their beauty. So that I, more or less unaware why I was brought there, and trusting the person who had led a friend of his to the brink of death, said to him: "Why have we come to see these women?" Then he replied: "To make sure they are worthily served." And the fact is that they were assembled there in the company of a gentlewoman who had been married that day; and so, in accordance with the customs of the aforesaid city, it behooved them to accompany her when she first sat down to table in the home of her new husband. And so I, thinking to please that friend, decided to remain and do homage to the women who accompanied her. But right after making that decision, I thought I felt a remarkable trembling which began on the left side of my chest and immediately spread all over my body. Then, I say, I surreptitiously rested my body against a fresco that ran all around that house; and fearing lest the others notice my trembling, I raised my eyes and, looking at the women, saw among them the most noble Beatrice. Then my spirits were so overcome by the strength which Love acquired, finding himself so close to that most noble lady, that only my spirits of sight remained active; and even they remained outside their organs, because Love insisted on taking their most excellent place in order to view that wonderful lady. And though I was in an altered state, I felt very sorry for those little spirits, which were loudly lamenting and saying: "If that fellow had not driven us out of our place this way, as if by lightning, we would be able to gaze on the marvel of that lady just as the others, our equals, are doing." To continue: many of those women, noticing my alteration, began to marvel, and in their talk made fun of me to that most noble lady; so that my friend, puzzled in good faith, took me by the hand and, leading me out of sight of those women, asked me what was wrong with me. Then,

mi domandò che io avesse. Allora io, riposato alquanto, e resurressiti
li morti spiriti miei, e li discacciati rivenuti a le loro possessioni, dissi
a questo mio amico queste parole: «Io tenni li piedi in quella parte de
la vita di là da la quale non si puote ire più per intendimento di ri-
tornare». E partitomi da lui, mi ritornai ne la camera de le lagrime; ne
la quale, piangendo e vergognandomi, fra me stesso dicea: «Se questa
donna sapesse la mia condizione, io non credo che così gabbasse la
mia persona, anzi credo che molta pietade le ne verrebbe». E in
questo pianto stando, propuosi di dire parole, ne le quali, parlando a
lei, significasse la cagione del mio trasfiguramento, e dicesse che io so
bene ch'ella non è saputa, e che se fosse saputa, io credo che pietà ne
giugnerebbe altrui; e propuosile di dire desiderando che venissero per
avventura ne la sua audienza. E allora dissi questo sonetto, lo quale
comincia: *Con l'altre donne*.

        Con l'altre donne mia vista gabbate,
            e non pensate, donna, onde si mova
            ch' io vi rassembri sì figura nova
            quando riguardo la vostra beltate.
        Se lo saveste, non poria Pietate
            tener più contra me l'usata prova,
            chè Amor, quando sì presso a voi mi trova,
            prende baldanza e tanta securtate,
    che fere tra'miei spiriti paurosi,
            e quale ancide, e qual pinge di fore,
            sì che solo remane a veder vui:
            ond'io mi cangio in figura d'altrui,
            ma non sì ch'io non senta bene allore
            li guai de li scacciati tormentosi.

Questo sonetto non divido in parti, però che la divisione non si fa se
non per aprire la sentenzia de la cosa divisa; onde con ciò sia cosa che
per la sua ragionata cagione assai sia manifesto, non ha mestiere di di-
visione. Vero è che tra le parole dove si manifesta la cagione di questo
sonetto, si scrivono dubbiose parole, cioè quando dico che Amore
uccide tutti li miei spiriti, e li visivi rimangono in vita, salvo che fuori
de li strumenti loro. E questo dubbio è impossibile a solvere a chi non
fosse in simile grado fedele d'Amore; e a coloro che vi sono è mani-
festo ciò che solverebbe le dubitose parole: e però non è bene a me di
dichiarare cotale dubitazione, acciò che lo mio parlare dichiarando
sarebbe indarno, o vero di soperchio.

XV. Appresso la nuova trasfigurazione mi giunse uno pensamento

after some rest, when my deadened spirits had been restored and the
dislodged ones had regained their possessions, I spoke these words to
my friend: "My feet were at the edge of life beyond which one cannot
pass with an expectation of returning." And taking leave of him, I re-
turned to my chamber of tears, in which, weeping and ashamed, I
kept saying to myself: "If that lady knew what a state I was in, I do not
think she would mock me as she did, but rather would take great pity
on me." And weeping that way, I resolved to write a poem in which,
addressing her, I would declare the reason for my alteration and say
that I was well aware that the reason was unknown, because if it were
known, I believe that others would feel pity; and I resolved to write it
with the desire that it might chance to reach her ears. Then I wrote
this sonnet, which begins "With the other women."

> With the other women you make fun of how I look,
>   my lady, and you take no thought of the reason
>   why I appear so odd to you
>   when I behold your beauty.
>   If you knew, Pity would no longer
>   be able to try me as she usually does,
>   because Love, when he finds me so close to you,
>   becomes cocky and so self-assured
> that he strikes blows among my timorous spirits,
>   killing some and driving others out,
>   so that he alone remains to gaze on you:
>   whereby I am changed into a different semblance,
>   but not so much that I am not still well aware
>   of the distress of the tortured dislodged spirits.

This sonnet I do not divide into parts, because division is made only
to clarify the meaning of the thing divided; so that, inasmuch as the
sonnet is quite clear from the background I have narrated, it has no
need of division. It is true that, among the phrases explaining the rea-
son for this sonnet, there are some difficult ones—that is, where I say
that Love kills all my spirits, but the spirits of sight remain alive,
although outside their organs. And this difficulty is impossible to over-
come for anyone who is not a faithful devotee of Love to the same
degree; whereas to those who have reached that degree, the solution
of the difficult passage is clear; therefore, it does not behoove me to
explain that difficulty, because my explanation would be either futile
or superfluous.

XI. After my odd alteration, a powerful thought came to me which

forte, lo quale poco si partia da me, anzi continuamente mi riprendea, ed era di cotale ragionamento meco: «Poscia che tu pervieni a così dischernevole vista quando tu se'presso di questa donna, perchè pur cerchi di vedere lei? Ecco che tu fossi domandato da lei: che avrestù da rispondere, ponendo che tu avessi libera ciascuna tua vertude in quanto tu le rispondessi?». E a costui rispondea un altro, umile, pensero, e dicea: «S'io non perdessi le mie vertudi, e fossi libero tanto che io le potessi rispondere, io le direi, che sì tosto com'io imagino la sua mirabile bellezza, sì tosto mi giugne uno desiderio di vederla, lo quale è di tanta vertude, che uccide e distrugge ne la mia memoria ciò che contra lui si potesse levare; e però non mi ritraggono le passate passioni da cercare la veduta di costei». Onde io, mosso da cotali pensamenti, propuosi di dire certe parole, ne le quali, escusandomi a lei da cotale riprensione, ponesse anche di quello che mi diviene presso di lei; e dissi questo sonetto, lo quale comincia: *Ciò che m'incontra*.

> Ciò che m'incontra, ne la mente more,
> quand'i'vegno a veder voi, bella gioia;
> e quand'io vi son presso, i'sento Amore
> che dice: «Fuggi, se 'l perir t'è noia».
> Lo viso mostra lo color del core,
> che, tramortendo, ovunque pò s'appoia;
> e per la ebrietà del gran tremore
> le pietre par che gridin: Moia, moia.
> Peccato face chi allora mi vide,
> se l'alma sbigottita non conforta,
> sol dimostrando che di me li doglia,
> per la pietà, che 'l vostro gabbo ancide,
> la qual si cria ne la vista morta
> de li occhi, c'hanno di lor morte voglia.

Questo sonetto si divide in due parti: ne la prima dico la cagione per che non mi tengo di gire presso di questa donna; ne la seconda dico quello che mi diviene per andare presso di lei; e comincia questa parte quivi: *e quand'io vi son presso*. E anche si divide questa seconda parte in cinque, secondo cinque diverse narrazioni: che ne la prima dico quello che Amore, consigliato da la ragione, mi dice quando le sono presso; ne la seconda manifesto lo stato del cuore per essemplo del viso; ne la terza dico sì come onne sicurtade mi viene meno; ne la quarta dico che pecca quelli che non mostra pietà di me, acciò che mi sarebbe alcuno conforto; ne l'ultima dico perchè altri doverebbe avere pietà, e ciò è per la pietosa vista che ne li occhi mi giugne; la quale

scarcely left me, but continually occupied me, and it was a self-address as follows: "Since you end up looking so ridiculous when you are near that lady, why do you still try to see her? If you were asked this by her, what would you reply, assuming that all your faculties were available to you while you replied?" And that thought was answered by another, humble one, which said: "If I did not lose my faculties, and were free for the time it took to reply, I would tell her that, as soon as her wondrous beauty comes to my mind, I feel a desire to see her which is so powerful that it kills and destroys in my memory whatever objections could be raised to it; therefore my past sufferings do not restrain me from seeking out the sight of her." And so, stirred by such thoughts, I resolved to write a poem in which, apologizing to her for my earlier reproach, I would also mention what happens to me when near her; and I wrote this sonnet, which begins "That which opposes me."

> That which opposes me dies away in my mind
>   when I happen to see you, beautiful jewel;
>   and when I am near you, I hear Love
>   saying: "Flee, if death displeases you!"
> My face shows the color of my heart,
>   which, swooning, supports itself wherever it can;
>   and in the intoxication of my great trembling
>   the stones seem to cry out: "Let him die, let him die!"
> Whoever sees me at such times commits a sin
>   if he does not comfort my dismayed soul,
>   merely showing that he is sorry for me,
>   out of compassion, which your mockery slays,
>   and which is aroused by the dead powers
>   of my eyes, which desire their own death.

This sonnet is divided into two parts: in the first, I state the reason why I do not refrain from seeking the proximity of that lady; in the second, I tell what happens to me when going near her; and this part begins with the words "and when I am near you." And this second part, in turn, is divided into five, according to five different statements: in the first of these I tell what Love, counseled by reason, says to me when I am near her; in the second, I declare the state of my heart as shown by my face; in the third, I tell how all my self-confidence abandons me; in the fourth, I say that whoever fails to show pity for me by giving me some comfort is committing a sin; in the last, I tell why people ought to have pity—because of the pitiful

vista pietosa è distrutta, cioè non pare altrui, per lo gabbare di questa donna, la quale trae a sua simile operazione coloro che forse vederebbono questa pietà. La seconda parte comincia quivi: *Lo viso mostra;* la terza quivi: *e per la ebrietà;* la quarta: *Peccato face;* la quinta: *per la pietà.*

XVI. Appresso ciò, che io dissi questo sonetto, mi mosse una volontade di dire anche parole, ne le quali io dicesse quattro cose ancora sopra lo mio stato, le quali non mi parea che fossero manifestate ancora per me. La prima delle quali si è che molte volte io mi dolea, quando la mia memoria movesse la fantasia ad imaginare quale Amore mi facea. La seconda si è che Amore spesse volte di subito m'assalia sì forte, che 'n me non rimanea altro di vita se non un pensero che parlava di questa donna. La terza si è che quando questa battaglia d'Amore mi pugnava così, io mi movea quasi discolorito tutto per vedere questa donna, credendo che mi difendesse la sua veduta da questa battaglia, dimenticando quello che per appropinquare a tanta gentilezza m'addivenia. La quarta si è come cotale veduta non solamente non mi difendea, ma finalmente disconfiggea la mia poca vita. E però dissi questo sonetto, lo quale comincia: *Spesse fiate.*

> Spesse fiate vegnonmi a la mente
>   le oscure qualità ch'Amor mi dona,
>   e venmene pietà, sì che sovente
>   io dico: «Lasso!, avviene elli a persona?»;
>   ch'Amor m'assale subitanamente,
>   sì che la vita quasi m'abbandona:
>   campami un spirto vivo solamente,
>   e que'riman, perchè di voi ragiona.
> Poscia mi sforzo, chè mi voglio atare;
>   e così smorto, d'onne valor voto,
>   vegno a vedervi, credendo guerire:
>   e se io levo li occhi per guardare,
>   nel cor mi si comincia uno tremoto.
>   che fa de'polsi l'anima partire.

Questo sonetto si divide in quattro parti, secondo che quattro cose sono in esso narrate; e però che sono di sopra ragionate, non m'intrametto se non di distinguere le parti per li loro cominciamenti: onde dico che la seconda parte comincia quivi: *ch'Amor;* la terza quivi: *Poscia mi sforzo;* la quarta quivi: *e se io levo.*

XVII. Poi che dissi questi tre sonetti, ne li quali parlai a questa donna, però che fuoro narratori di tutto quasi lo mio stato, creden-

look that comes into my eyes. That pitiful look is destroyed—that is, cannot be seen by others—by that woman's mockery, which leads those to mock me also who might otherwise acknowledge that pity. The second part begins with the words "my face shows"; the third, with "and in the intoxication"; the fourth, with "Whoever sees me"; the fifth, with "out of compassion."

XVI. After I wrote that sonnet, I felt the desire to write another poem in which I would make four statements about my condition which I thought had not yet been made by me. The first of them is that I was often grieved when my mind stirred my imagination to picture the state Love was reducing me to. The second is that often Love assailed me so violently all at once that all that remained alive in me was a thought that spoke of that lady. The third is that, when that assault of Love struggled with me that way, I went, almost entirely pale, to see that lady, thinking that the sight of her would protect me from that assault, and forgetting what happened to me when I approached such great nobility. The fourth is that such sights of her not only failed to protect me, but finally defeated the little life remaining to me. And so I wrote this sonnet, which begins "Frequently."

> Frequently there come to my mind
>   the puzzling characteristics Love gives me,
>   and I feel pity for them, so that often
>   I say: "Alas! Does this happen to anyone else?"
> Because Love assails me suddenly
>   in such a way that life nearly deserts me:
>   one living spirit alone is left to me,
>   and that one remains because it speaks of you.
> Then I make an effort, because I want to defend myself;
>   and thus, wan and drained of all strength,
>   I come to see you, thinking I will recover:
>   but if I raise my eyes to look at you,
>   such a great trembling begins in my heart
>   that it makes my soul desert my heartbeats.

This sonnet is divided into four parts, accordingly as four statements are made in it; but because they are spelled out above, I linger here merely to distinguish the parts by their beginnings; and so I say that the second part begins with the words "Because Love"; the third, with "Then I make an effort"; the fourth, with "but if I raise."

XVII. After I wrote those three sonnets addressing that lady, inasmuch as they were a declaration of nearly my complete condition, I

domi tacere e non dire più, però che mi parea di me assai avere manifestato, avvegna che sempre poi tacesse di dire a lei, a me convenne ripigliare matera nuova e più nobile che la passata. E però che la cagione de la nuova matera è dilettevole a udire, la dicerò, quanto potrò più brievemente.

XVIII. Con ciò sia cosa che per la vista mia molte persone avessero compreso lo secreto del mio cuore, certe donne, le quali adunate s'erano dilettandosi l'una ne la compagnia de l'altra, sapeano bene lo mio cuore, però che ciascuna di loro era stata a molte mie sconfitte; e io passando appresso di loro, sì come da la fortuna menato, fui chiamato da una di queste gentili donne. La donna che m'avea chiamato era donna di molto leggiadro parlare; sì che quand'io fui giunto dinanzi da loro, e vidi bene che la mia gentilissima donna non era con esse, rassicurandomi le salutai, e domandai che piacesse loro. Le donne erano molte, tra le quali n'avea certe che si rideano tra loro. Altre v'erano che mi guardavano, aspettando che io dovessi dire. Altre v'erano che parlavano tra loro. De le quali una, volgendo li suoi occhi verso me e chiamandomi per nome, disse queste parole: «A che fine ami tu questa tua donna, poi che tu non puoi sostenere la sua presenza? Dilloci, chè certo lo fine di cotale amore conviene che sia novissimo». E poi che m'ebbe dette queste parole, non solamente ella, ma tutte l'altre cominciaro ad attendere in vista la mia risponsione. Allora dissi queste parole loro: «Madonne, lo fine del mio amore fue già lo saluto di questa donna, forse di cui voi intendete, e in quello dimorava la beatitudine, chè era fine di tutti li miei desiderii. Ma poi che le piacque di negarlo a me, lo mio segnore Amore, la sua merzede, ha posto tutta la mia beatitudine in quello che non mi puote venire meno». Allora queste donne cominciaro a parlare tra loro; e sì come talora vedemo cadere l'acqua mischiata di bella neve, così mi parea udire le loro parole uscire mischiate di sospiri. E poi che alquanto ebbero parlato tra loro, anche mi disse questa donna che m'avea prima parlato, queste parole: «Noi ti preghiamo che tu ne dichi ove sta questa tua beatitudine». Ed io, rispondendo lei, dissi cotanto: «In quelle parole che lodano la donna mia». Allora mi rispuose questa che mi parlava: «Se tu ne dicessi vero, quelle parole che tu n'hai dette in notificando la tua condizione, avrestù operate con altro intendimento». Onde io, pensando a queste parole, quasi vergognoso mi partio da loro, e venia dicendo fra me medesimo: «Poi che è tanta beatitudine in quelle parole che lodano la mia donna, perchè altro parlare è stato lo mio?» E però proposi di prendere per matera de lo mio parlare sempre mai quello che fosse loda di questa gentilissima; e pen-

intended to be silent and say no more, thinking I had revealed enough of myself, even though I always afterward took care not to speak to her. I was now compelled to take up new subject matter, more noble than the earlier one. And because the reason for this new matter is pleasant to hear, I shall state it, as briefly as I can.

XVIII. Inasmuch as from my appearance many people had understood the secret of my heart, certain women who had assembled out of pleasure in one another's company were well aware of my affections, because each of them had been present at my many defeats; and I, passing by them, as if guided by Fortune, was called by one of those gentlewomen. The woman who had called to me was a woman of very charming speech; so that when I had arrived before them and ascertained that my most noble lady was not among them, I took heart and greeted them, asking what their pleasure was. The women were numerous, and some of them were laughing together. There were others who were looking at me, waiting for what I would say. There were others who were talking to one another. One of these, turning her eyes toward me and calling me by name, spoke these words: "To what end do you love this lady of yours, seeing that you cannot endure her presence? Tell us, because the goal of such a love must certainly be a great novelty." And after she addressed those words to me, not only she but all the others as well began to await my reply quite evidently. Then I spoke these words to them: "Ladies, the goal of my love used to be the greeting from that lady (perhaps you know whom I mean), and in that consisted the bliss which was the goal of all my desires. But ever since it has pleased her to deny it to me, my master, Love (and I thank him), has placed all my bliss in something which cannot fail me." Then those women began to speak with one another; and just as we sometimes see rain falling mixed with beautiful snow, thus I thought I heard their words issue mingled with sighs. And after they spoke together for a while, the same woman who had addressed me before spoke these words to me: "We beg you to tell us where this bliss of yours is located." And I, answering her, said this: "In those words which praise my lady." Then my female interlocutor replied: "If you were telling us the truth, you would have used with a different intention the words that you spoke to us when declaring your condition." Whereupon I, thinking of those words, parted from them almost in shame, and came away saying to myself: "Since there is such bliss in the words that praise my lady, why did I speak in other terms?" And so I resolved to adopt as the matter of my speech forever after whatever tended toward the praise of that most noble lady; and pondering this for some

sando molto a ciò, pareami avere impresa troppo alta matera quanto a me, sì che non ardia di cominciare; e così dimorai alquanti dì con disiderio di dire e con paura di cominciare.

XIX. Avvenne poi che passando per uno cammino lungo lo quale sen gia uno rivo chiaro molto, a me giunse tanta volontade di dire, che io cominciai a pensare lo modo ch'io tenesse; e pensai che parlare di lei non si convenia che io facesse, se io non parlasse a donne in seconda persona, e non ad ogni donna, ma solamente a coloro che sono gentili e che non sono pure femmine. Allora dico che la mia lingua parlò quasi come per se stessa mossa, e disse: *Donne ch'avete intelletto d'amore*. Queste parole io ripuosi ne la mente con grande letizia, pensando di prenderle per mio cominciamento; onde poi, ritornato a la sopradetta cittad, pensando alquanti die, cominciai una canzone con questo cominciamento, ordinata nel modo che si vedrà di sotto ne la sua divisione. La canzone comincia: *Donne ch'avete*.

> Donne ch'avete intelletto d'amore,
>   i'vo'con voi de la mia donna dire,
>   non perch'io creda sua laude finire,
>   ma ragionar per isfogar la mente.
>   Io dico che pensando il suo valore,
>   Amor sì dolce mi si fa sentire,
>   che s'io allora non perdessi ardire,
>   farei parlando innamorar la gente.
>   E io non vo' parlar sì altamente,
>   ch'io divenisse per temenza vile;
>   ma tratterò del suo stato gentile
>   a respetto di lei leggeramente,
>   donne e donzelle amorose, con vui,
>   chè non è cosa da parlarne altrui.
> Angelo clama in divino intelletto
>   e dice: «Sire, nel mondo si vede
>   maraviglia ne l'atto che procede
>   d'un'anima che 'nfin qua su risplende».
>   Lo cielo, che non have altro difetto
>   che d'aver lei, al suo segnor la chiede,
>   e ciascun santo ne grida merzede.
>   Sola Pietà nostra parte difende,
>   che parla Dio, che di madonna intende:
>   «Diletti miei, or sofferite in pace
>   che vostra spene sia quanto me piace

time, I felt that I had undertaken a matter too lofty for me, so that I did not dare to begin; so for several days I remained with the desire to speak and the fear of beginning.

XIX. It then befell that, walking down a road beside which a very clear stream was flowing, I felt such an urge to make an utterance that I began to think about how to go about it; and I decided that it did not behoove me to speak about her unless I addressed a number of women in the second person: not just any women, but only those who are of noble character and not merely females. Then, I say, my tongue spoke as if spontaneously, and said: "Ladies who have an understanding of love." I stored those words in my mind with great joy, intending to use them as my opening line; so that, later, having returned to the aforesaid city, and reflecting for several days, I started an ode beginning that way and organized in the manner that will be seen below when I divide it into parts. The ode begins: "Ladies who have."

Ladies who have an understanding of love,
    I wish to speak with you about my lady,
    not because I think I can exhaust her praises,
    but to talk and so relieve my mind.
    I say that, when I consider her worth,
    Love makes himself felt to me so sweetly
    that, if I did not lose courage then,
    I would make everyone fall in love as I spoke.
    And I do not wish to speak so loftily
    as to become cowardly through fear;
    but I shall discuss her noble condition
    only slightly, as regards her merit,
    with you, loving ladies and maidens,
    for it is not a subject to discuss with others.
An angel cries out to the Divine Mind,
    saying: "Lord, in the world is seen
    a marvel in the actions which proceed
    from a soul whose glow reaches all the way up here."
    Heaven, which has no other lack
    than the lack of her, demands her of its Lord,
    and every saint calls for that favor.
    Only Pity takes our part,
    when God speaks, with my lady in mind:
    "My beloved ones, now endure in peace
    that your hope be deferred until it is my pleasure,

là 'v'è alcun che perder lei s'attende,
e che dirà ne lo inferno: O mal nati,
io vidi la speranza de'beati».
Madonna è disiata in sommo cielo:
or voi di sua virtù farvi savere.
Dico, qual vuol gentil donna parere
vada con lei, che quando va per via,
gitta nei cor villani Amore un gelo,
per che onne lor pensero agghiaccia e pere;
e qual soffrisse di starla a vedere
diverria nobil cosa, o si morria.
E quando trova alcun che degno sia
di veder lei, quei prova sua vertute,
chè li avvien, ciò che li dona, in salute,
e sì l'umilia, ch'ogni offesa oblia.
Ancor l'ha Dio per maggior grazia dato
che non pò mal finir chi l'ha parlato.
Dice di lei Amor: «Cosa mortale
come esser pò sì adorna e sì pura?».
Poi la reguarda, e fra se stesso giura
che Dio ne 'ntenda di far cosa nova.
Color di perle ha quasi, in forma quale
convene a donna aver, non for misura:
ella è quanto de ben pò far natura;
per essemplo di lei bieltà si prova.
De li occhi suoi, come ch'ella li mova,
escono spirti d'amore inflammati,
che feron li occhi a qual che allor la guati,
e passan sì che 'l cor ciascun retrova:
voi le vedete Amor pinto nel viso,
là 've non pote alcun mirarla fiso.
Canzone, io so che tu girai parlando
a donne assai, quand'io t'avrò avanzata.
Or t'ammonisco, perch'io t'ho allevata
per figliuola d'Amor giovane e piana,
che là 've giugni tu dichi pregando:
«Insegnatemi gir, ch'io son mandata
a quella di cui laude so'adornata».
E se non vuoli andar sì come vana,
non restare ove sia gente villana:
ingegnati, se puoi, d'esser palese

for there is a man there who expects to lose her
and who will say in the Inferno: "O souls of the damned,
I have seen the hope of the souls in bliss.'"
My lady is desired in the highest heaven:
now I wish to inform you of her virtue.
I say: whoever of you wants to appear as a gentlewoman
should go with her, for when she walks abroad
Love casts a chill into base hearts,
making their every thought freeze and perish;
and whoever could endure standing there and beholding her
would become something noble, or would die.
And when she finds someone who would be worthy
of beholding her, that person experiences her virtue,
because what she gives him redounds to his salvation,
and humbles him so, that he forgets every offense.
Also, God has granted her the even greater favor
that whoever has spoken with her cannot be damned.
Love says of her: "How can a mortal creature
be so beautiful and yet so pure?"
Then he looks at her again, and swears to himself
that God meant to create something new in her.
Her color is nearly that of pearls, her form such
as it behooves woman to have, not immoderate:
she is the highest good that nature can make;
beauty is tested with her as the touchstone.
From her eyes, whenever she moves them,
issue flaming spirits of love
which smite the eyes of whoever looks upon her then,
and they pierce so well that each one reaches the heart:
you see Love depicted on her lips,
which no one can behold steadily.
Ode, I know that you will roam about speaking
to many women after I have launched you.
Now I admonish you, since I have raised you
as a young, modest daughter of Love,
that, wherever you go, you make this request:
"Teach me where to go, for I have been sent
to her with whose praises I am adorned."
And if you do not want to go about like a silly idler,
do not linger in the company of base people:
strive, if you can, to open your heart

> solo con donne o con omo cortese,
> che ti merranno là per via tostana.
> Tu troverai Amor con esso lei;
> raccomandami a lui come tu dei.

Questa canzone, acció che sia meglio intesa, la dividerò più artifi-
ciosamente che l'altre cose di sopra. E però prima ne fo tre parti: la
prima parte è proemio de le sequenti parole; la seconda è lo intento
trattato; la terza è quasi una serviziale de le precedenti parole. La
seconda comincia quivi: *Angelo clama;* la terza quivi: *Canzone, io so
che.* La prima parte si divide in quattro: ne la prima dico a cu'io
dicer voglio de la mia donna, e perchè io voglio dire; ne la seconda
dico quale me pare avere a me stesso quand'io penso lo suo valore,
e com'io direi s'io non perdessi l'ardimento; ne la terza dico come
credo dire di lei, acciò ch'io non sia impedito da viltà; ne la quarta,
ridicendo anche a cui ne intenda dire, dico la cagione per che dico a
loro. La seconda comincia quivi: *Io dico;* la terza quivi: *E io non
vo'parlar;* la quarta: *donne e donzelle.* Poscia quando dico: *Angelo
clama,* comincio a trattare di questa donna. E dividesi questa parte
in due: ne la prima dico che di lei si comprende in cielo; ne la secon-
da dico che di lei si comprende in terra, quivi: *Madonna è disiata.*
Questa seconda parte si divide in due; che ne la prima dico di lei
quanto da la parte de la nobilitade de la sua anima, narrando
alquanto de le sue vertudi effettive che de la sua anima procedeano;
ne la seconda dico di lei quanto da la parte de la nobilitade del suo
corpo, narrando alquanto de le sue bellezze, quivi: *Dice di lei Amor.*
Questa seconda parte si divide in due; che ne la prima dico
d'alquante bellezze che sono secondo tutta la persona; ne la seconda
dico d'alquante bellezze che sono secondo diterminata parte de la
persona, quivi: *De li occhi suoi.* Questa seconda parte si divide in
due; che ne l'una dico degli occhi, li quali sono principio d'amore;
ne la seconda dico de la bocca, la quale è fine d'amore. E acciò che
quinci si lievi ogni vizioso pensiero, ricordisi chi ci legge, che di
sopra è scritto che lo saluto di questa donna, lo quale era de le ope-
razioni de la bocca sua, fue fine de li miei desiderii mentre ch'io lo
potei ricevere. Poscia quando dico: *Canzone, io so che tu,* aggiungo
una stanza quasi come ancella de l'altre, ne la quale dico quello che
di questa mia canzone desidero; e però che questa ultima parte è
lieve a intendere, non mi travaglio di più divisioni. Dico bene che, a
più aprire lo intendimento di questa canzone, si converrebbe usare
di più minute divisioni; ma tuttavia chi non è di tanto ingegno che

only to women or to a courteous man,
who will send you promptly on your path.
You will find Love with her;
commend me to him as is your duty.

So that this ode may be better understood, I shall divide it more com-
plexly than I did the preceding poems. And so I begin by making three
parts of it: the first part is the preamble to what follows; the second is the
subject matter treated; the third is, as it were, a servant to the earlier sec-
tions. The second begins with the words "An angel cries out"; the third,
with "Ode, I know that." The first part is itself subdivided into four: in
the first, I state to whom I wish to speak of my lady, and why I wish to
speak; in the second, I describe the condition I seem to be in when I
think of her worth, and what I would say if I did not lose my courage; in
the third, I say how I think I should speak about her in order not to be
hindered by cowardice; in the fourth, restating my intended audience, I
give the reason why I address them. The second of these subdivisions be-
gins with the words "I say"; the third, with "And I do not wish to speak";
the fourth, with "ladies and maidens." Then, when I say "An angel cries
out," I begin to treat of that lady. And this part is divided in two: in the
first, I state what is understood of her in heaven; in the second, I state
what is understood of her on earth, beginning with "My lady is desired."
This second part is further divided in two: in the first, I discuss her with
reference to the nobility of her soul, recounting a few of the active virtues
proceeding from her soul; in the second, I discuss her with reference to
the nobility of her body, recounting a few of her beauties, beginning with
"Love says of her." This second part is itself divided in two: in the first, I
mention some beauties that reside in her entire person; in the second, I
mention some beauties that reside in a specific part of her person, be-
ginning with "From her eyes." Even this second part is divided in two: in
the first, I mention her eyes, which are the outset of love; in the second,
I mention her lips, which are the end goal of love. And, so that every evil
thought may be removed from here, let my readers recall that it is writ-
ten above that this lady's greeting, which was among the functions of her
lips, was the goal of my desires for as long as I could receive it. Later,
when I say "Ode, I know that you," I add a stanza more or less ancillary
to the rest, in which I say what I want my ode to do; and because this last
part is easy to understand, I do not trouble myself with further divisions.
I do say that, to reveal the meaning of this ode even more, it would be
necessary to use smaller subdivisions; but, all the same, if there is some-
one insufficiently bright to be able to understand it by means of the di-

per queste che sono fatte la possa intendere, a me non dispiace se la
mi lascia stare, chè certo io temo d'avere a troppi comunicato lo suo
intendimento pur per queste divisioni che fatte sono, s'elli avvenisse
che molti le potessero audire.

XX. Appresso che questa canzone fue alquanto divolgata tra le
genti, con ciò fosse cosa che alcuno amico l'udisse, volontade lo mosse
a pregare me che io li dovesse dire che è Amore, avendo forse per l'u-
dite parole speranza di me oltre che degna. Onde io, pensando che
appresso di cotale trattato bello era trattare alquanto d'Amore, e pen-
sando che l'amico era da servire, propuosi di dire parole ne le quali io
trattassi d'Amore; e allora dissi questo sonetto, lo qual comincia:
Amore e 'l cor gentil.

> Amore e 'l cor gentil sono una cosa,
>   sì come il saggio in suo dittare pone,
>   e così esser l'un sanza l'altro osa
>   com'alma razional sanza ragione.
>   Falli natura quand'è amorosa,
>   Amor per sire e 'l cor per sua magione,
>   dentro la qual dormendo si riposa
>   tal volta poca e tal lunga stagione.
> Bieltate appare in saggia donna pui,
>   che piace a gli occhi sì, che dentro al core
>   nasce un disio de la cosa piacente;
>   e tanto dura talora in costui,
>   che fa svegliar lo spirito d'Amore.
>   E simil face in donna omo valente.

Questo sonetto si divide in due parti: ne la prima dico di lui in
quanto è in potenzia; ne la seconda dico di lui in quanto di potenzia si
riduce in atto. La seconda comincia quivi: *Bieltate appare.* La prima
si divide in due: ne la prima dico in che suggetto sia questa potenzia;
ne la seconda dico sì come questo suggetto e questa potenzia siano
produtti in essere, e come l'uno guarda l'altro come forma materia. La
seconda comincia quivi: *Falli natura.* Poscia quando dico: *Bieltate ap-
pare,* dico come questa potenzia si riduce in atto; e prima come si
riduce in uomo, poi come si riduce in donna, quivi: *E simil face in
donna.*

XXI. Poscia che trattai d'Amore ne la soprascritta rima, vennemi

visions already made, I will not be sorry if he puts the whole thing aside, because I surely fear I have communicated its meaning to all too many people already even with the few divisions I have made, should it come about that many people are able to hear it.

XX. After that ode had become somewhat widely known among my fellow citizens, when a certain friend of mine heard it, he conceived the desire to ask me to tell him what Love is, perhaps because the words he had heard gave him expectations that exceeded my powers. Wherefore, thinking that, after a treatise of that sort, it would be nice to treat somewhat of Love, and thinking that my friend ought to be obliged, I resolved to write a poem in which I would treat of Love; and then I wrote this sonnet, which begins: "Love and the noble heart."

> Love and the noble heart are one and the same thing,
>   as the sage[14] states in his poem,
>   and one of them dares as little to exist without the other
>   as does the rational soul without reasoning.
>   Nature creates them when she is in love,
>   Love as the master and the heart as his residence,
>   within which he reposes in slumber
>   sometimes briefly and sometimes for a long period.
> Then beauty appears in a knowing woman,
>   who so pleases the eye that within the heart
>   a desire for the pleasing thing arises;
>   and sometimes it lasts so long in the heart
>   that it awakens the spirit of Love.
>   And a worthy man does the same thing to a woman.

This sonnet is divided into two parts: in the first, I speak of Love in so far as he remains potential; in the second, I speak of him when his potentiality is converted into activity. The second begins with the words "Then beauty appears." The first part is subdivided in two: in the first, I say in what subject this potentiality resides; in the second, I tell how this subject and this potentiality become an essence, and how one is wed to the other as form is wed to matter. The second subdivision begins with the words "Nature creates them." Later, when I say "Then beauty appears," I tell how this potentiality is converted into activity; first, how it is converted in a man, then how it is converted in a woman, at the words "And a worthy man."

XXI. After I treated of Love in the aforesaid poem, I felt the fur-

---

14. Guido Guinizzelli.

volontade di volere dire anche, in loda di questa gentilissima, parole, per le quali io mostrasse come per lei si sveglia questo Amore, e come non solamente si sveglia là ove dorme, ma là ove non è in potenzia, ella, mirabilemente operando, lo fa venire. E allora dissi questo sonetto, lo quale comincia: *Ne li occhi porta.*

> Ne li occhi porta la mia donna Amore,
>> per che si fa gentil ciò ch'ella mira;
>> ov'ella passa, ogn'om ver lei si gira,
>> e cui saluta fa tremar lo core,
>>> sì che, bassando il viso, tutto smore,
>>> e d'ogni suo difetto allor sospira:
>>> fugge dinanzi a lei superbia ed ira.
>>> Aiutatemi, donne, farle onore.
> Ogne dolcezza, ogne pensero umile
>> nasce nel core a chi parlar la sente,
>> ond'è laudato chi prima la vide.
>>> Quel ch'ella par quando un poco sorride,
>>> non si pò dicer nè tenere a mente,
>>> sì è novo miracolo e gentile.

Questo sonetto si ha tre parti: ne la prima dico sì come questa donna riduce questa potenzia in atto secondo la nobilissima parte de li suoi occhi; e ne la terza dico questo medesimo secondo la nobilissima parte de la sua bocca; e intra queste due parti è una particella, ch'è quasi domandatrice d'aiuto a la precedente parte e a la sequente, e comincia quivi: *Aiutatemi, donne.* La terza comincia quivi: *Ogne dolcezza.* La prima si divide in tre; che ne la prima parte dico sì come virtuosamente fae gentile tutto ciò che vede, e questo è tanto a dire quanto inducere Amore in potenzia là ove non è; ne la seconda dico come reduce in atto Amore ne li cuori di tutti coloro cui vede; ne la terza dico quello che poi virtuosamente adopera ne' loro cuori. La seconda comincia quivi: *ov'ella passa;* la terza quivi: *e cui saluta.* Poscia quando dico: *Aiutatemi, donne,* do a intendere a cui la mia intenzione è di parlare, chiamando le donne che m'aiutino onorare costei. Poscia quando dico: *Ogne dolcezza,* dico quello medesimo che detto è ne la prima parte, secondo due atti de la sua bocca; l'uno de li quali è lo suo dolcissimo parlare, e l'altro lo suo mirabile riso; salvo che non dico di questo ultimo come adopera ne li cuori altrui, però che la memoria non puote ritenere lui nè sua operazione.

XXII. Appresso ciò non molti dì passati, sì come piacque al glorioso sire lo quale non negoe la morte a sè, colui che era stato genitore di

ther urge to write a poem in praise of that most noble lady, in which I would show how this Love is awakened by her, and how he is not only awakened where he lies sleeping, but how, even there where he does not potentially reside, she makes him arrive by her miraculous working. And then I wrote this sonnet, which begins: "In her eyes."

> In her eyes my lady bears Love,
>> through whom whatever she beholds is ennobled;
>> wherever she goes, every man turns in her direction,
>> and every man's heart trembles whom she greets,
>> so that, lowering his face, he turns completely pale,
>> and then sighs for all that he lacks:
>> haughtiness and wrath flee before her.
>> Help me, ladies, to honor her.
> Every sweetness, every humble thought
>> arises in the heart of him who hears her speak,
>> so that he who first sees her is praised.
>> How she looks when she gives a little smile
>> cannot be uttered or retained in mind,
>> it is such a strange and noble miracle.

This sonnet has three parts: in the first, I tell how this lady converts that potentiality into activity by means of those most noble organs, her eyes; in the third, I say the same with regard to those most noble features, her lips; and between those two parts there is a brief one which, as it were, requests aid from the parts that precede and follow it; it begins with "Help me, ladies." The third begins with "Every sweetness." The first part is subdivided in three: in the first part I tell how by her virtue she ennobles all that she sees, which is equivalent to saying that she introduces Love in potentiality to places he does not yet reside in; in the second, I tell how she converts Love into activity in the hearts of all those whom she beholds; in the third, I tell what she then brings to pass in their hearts by her virtue. The second subdivision begins with "wherever she goes"; the third, with "and every man's heart." Later, when I say "Help me, ladies," I make it clear whom I intend to address, calling upon the ladies to help me honor her. Later, when I say "Every sweetness," I say the same thing as stated in the first part, with regard to two actions of her lips, one of them being her very sweet speech, and the other her remarkable smile; except that I do not say how the latter affects other people's hearts, because the mind cannot grasp it or its effect.

XXII. Not many days after that, as it pleased the glorious Lord who did not refuse to take death upon himself, the man who had begotten

tanta meraviglia quanta si vedea ch'era questa nobilissima Beatrice, di
questa vita uscendo, a la gloria etternale se ne gio veracemente. Onde
con ciò sia cosa che cotale partire sia doloroso a coloro che rimangono
e sono stati amici di colui che se ne va; e nulla sia sì intima amistade
come da buon padre a buon figliuolo e da buon figliuolo a buon padre;
e questa donna fosse in altissimo grado di bontade, e lo suo padre, sì
come da molti si crede e vero è, fosse bono in alto grado; manifesto è
che questa donna fue amarissimamente piena di dolore. E con ciò sia
cosa che, secondo l'usanza de la sopradetta cittade, donne con donne
e uomini con uomini s'adunino a cotale tristizia, molte donne
s'adunaro colà dove questa Beatrice piangea pietosamente: onde io
veggendo ritornare alquante donne da lei, udio dicere loro parole di
questa gentilissima, com'ella si lamentava; tra le quali parole udio che
diceano: «Certo ella piange sì, che quale la mirasse doverebbe morire
di pietade». Allora trapassaro queste donne; e io rimasi in tanta tri-
stizia, che alcuna lagrima talora bagnava la mia faccia, onde io mi rico-
pria con porre le mani spesso a li miei occhi; e se non fosse ch'io
attendea audire anche di lei, però ch'io era in luogo onde se ne giano
la maggiore parte di quelle donne che da lei si partiano, io mi sarei
nascoso incontanente che le lagrime m'aveano assalito. E però di-
morando ancora nel medesimo luogo, donne anche passaro presso di
me, le quali andavano ragionando tra loro queste parole: «Chi dee mai
essere lieta di noi, che avemo udita parlare questa donna così pietosa-
mente?». Appresso costoro passaro altre donne, che veniano dicendo:
«Questi ch'è qui piange nè più nè meno come se l'avesse veduta, come
noi avemo». Altre dipoi diceano di me: «Vedi questi che non pare esso,
tal è divenuto!». E così passando queste donne, udio parole di lei e di
me in questo modo che detto è. Onde io poi, pensando, propuosi di
dire parole, acciò che degnamente avea cagione di dire, ne le quali pa-
role io conchiudesse tutto ciò che inteso avea da queste donne; e però
che volentieri l'averei domandate, se non mi fosse stata riprensione,
presi tanta matera di dire come s'io l'avesse domandate ed elle
m'avessero risposto. E feci due sonetti; che nel primo domando in
quello modo che voglia mi giunse di domandare; ne l'altro dico la loro
risponsione, pigliando ciò ch'io udio da loro sì come lo mi avessero
detto rispondendo. E comincia lo primo: *Voi che portate la sembianza
umile*, e l'altro: *Se'tu colui c'hai trattato sovente*.

> Voi che portate la sembianza umile,
>   con li occhi bassi, mostrando dolore,
>   onde venite che 'l vostro colore

the great marvel which that most noble Beatrice was seen to be, departed from this life, and surely went to eternal glory. Therefore, inasmuch as such separations are painful to those left behind who were friends of the departed, and there is no closer friendship than a good father's for a good child and a good child's for a good father, and that lady was good in the highest degree, and her father, as many believe, and rightly so, was good in a high degree, it is obvious that that lady was filled with bitter grief. And inasmuch as, in accordance with the customs of the aforesaid city, women join with women, and men with men, on such sad occasions, many women assembled where Beatrice was weeping compassionately; so that, when I saw several women returning from her house, I overheard their words concerning that most noble lady, about how she was lamenting; among those words I heard them say: "Truly, she is weeping so hard that anyone beholding her ought to die of pity." Then those women went by, and I was left so sad that tears wet my face at times, which I concealed by frequently putting my hand up to my eyes; and if I did not have hopes of hearing more about her, since I was in a place which most of the women leaving her home passed by, I would have hidden the moment that the tears assailed me. And while I was still in the same place for that reason, more women passed by me who were speaking to one another as follows: "Who among us can ever be happy, having heard that lady speak so compassionately?" Behind them came other women, who were saying: "This man here is weeping exactly as if he had seen her, as we have." Later, other women said about me: "Look at this man, who does not seem himself, he has been so altered!" And as those ladies went by in that way, I heard words about her and about me of the kind I have mentioned. So that, pondering this afterward, I resolved to write a poem (because I had a worthy cause to do so) in which I would include all I had heard those women say; and because I would gladly have questioned them, had it not involved a reproach to me, I used as much material as if I had questioned them and they had replied. And I wrote two sonnets; in the first, I question them in the way I had desired to do; in the second, I state their reply, using what I had heard them say as if they had said it to me in reply. And the first begins: "You whose bearing is humble"; and the second: "Are you the man who has often discussed."

> You whose bearing is humble,
>   your eyes cast down, displaying grief,
>   whence do you come that your coloring

par divenuto de pietà simile?
Vedeste voi nostra donna gentile
bagnar nel viso suo di pianto Amore?
Ditelmi, donne, che 'l mi dice il core,
perch'io vi veggio andar sanz'atto vile.
E se venite da tanta pietate,
piacciavi di restar qui meco alquanto,
e qual che sia di lei, nol mi celate.
Io veggio li occhi vostri c'hanno pianto,
e veggiovi tornar sì sfigurate,
che 'l cor mi triema di vederne tanto.

Questo sonetto si divide in due parti: ne la prima chiamo e domando queste donne se vegnono da lei, dicendo loro che io lo credo, però che tornano quasi ingentilite; ne la seconda le prego che mi dicano di lei. La seconda comincia quivi: *E se venite.*
Qui appresso è l'altro sonetto, sì come dinanzi avemo narrato.

Se'tu colui c'hai trattato sovente
di nostra donna, sol parlando a nui?
Tu risomigli a la voce ben lui,
ma la figura ne par d'altra gente.
E perchè piangi tu sì coralmente,
che fai di te pietà venire altrui?
Vedestù pianger lei, che tu non pui
punto celar la dolorosa mente?
Lascia piangere noi e triste andare
(e fa peccato chi mai ne conforta),
che nel suo pianto l'udimmo parlare.
Ell'ha nel viso la pietà sì scorta,
che qual l'avesse voluta mirare
sarebbe innanzi lei piangendo morta.

Questo sonetto ha quattro parti, secondo che quattro modi di parlare ebbero in loro le donne per cui rispondo; e però che sono di sopra assai manifesti, non m'intrametto di narrare la sentenzia de le parti, e però le distinguo solamente. La seconda comincia quivi: *E perchè piangi;* la terza: *Lascia piangere noi;* la quarta: *Ell'ha nel viso.*
XXIII. Appresso ciò per pochi dì avvenne che in alcuna parte de la mia persona mi giunse una dolorosa infermitade, onde io continuamente soffersi per nove dì amarissima pena; la quale mi condusse a

seems to have become an image of pity?
Did you see our noble lady
bathe Love with the tears on her face?
Tell me, ladies, for my heart tells me so,
since I see you walking free from baseness.
And if you are coming from a scene of such compassion,
please linger here with me awhile,
and do not conceal anything about her from me.
I see your eyes full of tears,
and I see you returning so discomposed
that my heart trembles to see so much.

This sonnet is divided into two parts: in the first, I call out and ask those women whether they are coming from her house, telling them that I believe that to be the case, because they are returning ennobled, so to speak; in the second, I beg them to talk to me about her. The second part begins with the words "And if you are coming."

Here, following, is the second sonnet, as I have recounted above.

Are you the man who has often discussed
our lady, speaking to us only?
Your voice does resemble his,
but your face seems like someone else's.
And why do you weep in such a heartfelt way
that you make others feel pity for you?
Did you see her weep, so that you cannot
at all conceal the sorrow in your mind?
Let *us* weep and go about sadly
(he commits a sin who ever consoles us),
for we have heard her speaking as she wept.
Compassion is so manifest in her face
that whoever of us had wanted to behold her
would have died weeping in her presence.

This sonnet has four parts, just as the ladies for whom I reply used four modes of speech; and because these have been made quite clear above, I do not linger to explain the meaning of the parts, but merely distinguish them. The second begins with the words "And why do you weep"; the third, with "Let *us* weep"; the fourth, with "Compassion is so manifest."

XXIII. A few days after that, it came about that in some part of my body I was afflicted by a painful ailment, so that I constantly suffered very grievous pain for nine days; this made me so weak that I had to

tanta debolezza, che me convenia stare come coloro li quali non si
possono muovere. Io dico che ne lo nono giorno, sentendome dolere
quasi intollerabilmente, a me giunse uno pensero lo quale era de la
mia donna. E quando ei pensato alquanto di lei, ed io ritornai pen-
sando a la mia debilitata vita; e veggendo come leggiero era lo suo du-
rare, ancora che sana fosse, sì cominciai a piangere fra me stesso di
tanta miseria. Onde, sospirando forte, dicea fra me medesimo: «Di
necessitade convene che la gentilissima Beatrice alcuna volta si
muoia». E però mi giunse uno sì forte smarrimento, che chiusi li occhi
e cominciai a travagliare sì come farnetica persona ed a imaginare in
questo modo: che ne lo incominciamento de lo errare che fece la mia
fantasia, apparvero a me certi visi di donne scapigliate, che mi
diceano: «Tu pur morrai». E poi, dopo queste donne, m'apparvero
certi visi diversi e orribili a vedere, li quali mi diceano: «Tu se'morto».
Così cominciando ad errare la mia fantasia, venni a quello ch'io non
sapea ove io mi fosse; e vedere mi parea donne andare scapigliate
piangendo per via, maravigliosamente triste; e pareami vedere lo sole
oscurare, sì che le stelle si mostravano di colore ch'elle mi faceano
giudicare che piangessero; e pareami che li uccelli volando per l'aria
cadessero morti, e che fossero grandissimi terremuoti. E maviglian-
domi in cotale fantasia, e paventando assai, imaginai alcuno amico che
mi venisse a dire: «Or non sai? la tua mirabile donna è partita di
questo secolo». Allora cominciai a piangere molto pietosamente; e
non solamente piangea ne la imaginazione, ma piangea con li occhi,
bagnandoli di vere lagrime. Io imaginava di guardare verso lo cielo, e
pareami vedere moltitudine d'angeli li quali tornassero in suso, ed
aveano dinanzi da loro una nebuletta bianchissima. A me parea che
questi angeli cantassero gloriosamente, e le parole del loro canto mi
parea udire che fossero queste: *Osanna in excelsis;* e altro non mi pa-
rea udire. Allora mi parea che lo cuore, ove era tanto amore, mi
dicesse: «Vero è che morta giace la nostra donna». E per questo mi
parea andare per vedere lo corpo ne lo quale era stata quella nobilis-
sima e beata anima; e fue sì forte la erronea fantasia, che mi mostrò
questa donna morta: e pareami che donne la covrissero, cioè la sua
testa, con uno bianco velo; e pareami che la sua faccia avesse tanto
aspetto d'umilitade, che parea che dicesse: «Io sono a vedere lo prin-
cipio de la pace». In questa imaginazione mi giunse tanta umilitade
per vedere lei, che io chiamava la Morte, e dicea: «Dolcissima Morte,
vieni a me, e non m'essere villana, però che tu dei essere gentile, in
tal parte se'stata! Or vieni a me, chè molto ti desidero; e tu lo vedi, chè
io porto già lo tuo colore». E quando io avea veduto compiere tutti li

remain like those who cannot stir themselves. I say that on the ninth day, feeling almost unbearable pain, I had a thought, which was of my lady. And after thinking of her for a while, I went back to pondering on my weakened condition; and seeing how brief the duration of my life was, even if I were healthy, I began to weep inwardly over such wretchedness. So that, sighing deeply, I said to myself: "Of necessity, the most noble Beatrice will have to die some day." And this brought on such a terrible confusion that I shut my eyes and began to be afflicted like a madman and to have the following kind of imaginings: at the outset of my mind's straying, there appeared to me certain faces of disheveled women who said to me: "You, too, will die." Then, after those women, there appeared to me certain faces, various and awful to behold, who said to me: "You are dead." My mind beginning to stray in that manner, I went so far as not knowing where I was; and I thought I saw disheveled women walking down the street in tears, wondrously sad; and I thought I saw the sun darken, so that the stars appeared in a color that made me imagine they were weeping; and I thought the birds flying through the air fell dead, and that there were very strong earth tremors. And in amazement at such fancies, and extremely frightened, I imagined that some friend came and told me: "Do you not know yet? Your remarkable lady has departed from this life." Then I began to weep very piteously; I was weeping not only in my imagination, but with my eyes, bathing them in actual tears. I thought I was looking up at heaven, and I thought I saw a multitude of angels returning up there, who had a very white little cloud in front of them. It seemed to me that those angels were singing gloriously, and I thought I heard the words of their chant to be these: "Hosanna in the highest"; and I seemed to hear nothing else. Then I thought that my heart, in which there was so much love, said to me: "It is true that our lady is lying dead." And therefore I thought I was going to view the body that had sheltered that most noble and blessed soul; and my fallacious imagining was so strong that it showed me that dead lady; and I thought that women were covering her (her head, that is) with a white veil; and I thought that her face had such a look of humility that it seemed to be saying: "I am now seeing the onset of peace." In that imagining, I was so filled with humility through seeing her that I called upon Death, saying: "Most sweet Death, come to me, and do not be cruel to me, because you must be gentle, seeing where you have been! Now come to me, for I desire you greatly; you see this because I am already wearing your color." And after I had seen performed all the sorrowful tasks which are customarily undertaken for

dolorosi mestieri che a le corpora de li morti s'usano di fare, mi parea tornare ne la mia camera, e quivi mi parea guardare verso lo cielo; e sì forte era la mia imaginazione, che piangendo incominciai a dire con verace voce: «Oi anima bellissima, come è beato colui che ti vede!». E dicendo io queste parole con doloroso singulto di pianto, e chiamando la Morte che venisse a me, una donna giovane e gentile, la quale era lungo lo mio letto, credendo che lo mio piangere e le mie parole fossero solamente per lo dolore de la mia infermitade, con grande paura cominciò a piangere. Onde altre donne che per la camera erano s'accorsero di me, che io piangea, per lo pianto che vedeano fare a questa; onde faccendo lei partire da me, la quale era meco di propinquissima sanguinitade congiunta, elle si trassero verso me per isvegliarmi, credendo che io sognasse, e diceanmi: «Non dormire più», e «Non ti sconfortare». E parlandomi così, sì mi cessò la forte fantasia entro in quello punto ch'io volea dicere: «O Beatrice, benedetta sie tu»; e già detto avea «O Beatrice», quando riscotendomi apersi li occhi, e vidi che io era ingannato. E con tutto che io chiamasse questo nome, la mia voce era sì rotta dal singulto del piangere, che queste donne non mi pottero intendere, secondo il mio parere; e avvegna che io vergognasse molto, tuttavia per alcuno ammonimento d'Amore mi rivolsi a loro. E quando mi videro, cominciaro a dire: «Questi pare morto», e a dire tra loro: «Procuriamo di confortarlo»; onde molte parole mi diceano da confortarmi, e talora mi domandavano di che io avesse avuto paura. Onde io, essendo alquanto riconfortato, e conosciuto lo fallace imaginare, rispuosi a loro: «Io vi diroe quello ch'i' hoe avuto». Allora, cominciandomi dal principio infino a la fine, dissi loro quello che veduto avea, tacendo lo nome di questa gentilissima. Onde poi, sanato di questa infermitade, propuosi di dire parole di questo che m'era addivenuto, però che mi parea che fosse amorosa cosa da udire; e però ne dissi questa canzone: *Donna pietosa e di novella etate*, ordinata sì come manifesta la infrascritta divisione.

> Donna pietosa e di novella etate,
>   adorna assai di gentilezze umane,
>   ch'era là 'v'io chiamava spesso Morte,
>   veggendo li occhi miei pien di pietate,
>   e ascoltando le parole vane,
>   si mosse con paura a pianger forte.
>   E altre donne, che si fuoro accorte
>   di me per quella che meco piangia,
>   fecer lei partir via,

the bodies of the dead, I thought I returned to my chamber, and there
I thought I looked up to heaven; and my imagining was so strong that,
weeping, I began to say in truthful tones: "Ah, most beautiful soul,
how blessed is he who sees you!" And when I spoke those words with
sorrowful sobbing and weeping, and called upon Death to come to
me, a young, kind lady who was at my bedside, thinking my tears and
words stemmed merely from the pain of my ailment, began to weep
in great fear. So that other women who were in the room became
aware I was weeping when they noticed the tears that *she* was shed-
ding; whereupon, making her leave me (she was a very close blood re-
lation of mine), they drew near me to awaken me, thinking I was
dreaming, and they said: "Sleep no longer," and "Do not despair." And
when they addressed me thus, my strong imagining ceased just when
I was about to say: "O Beatrice, be blessed"; I had already uttered "O
Beatrice," when, rousing myself, I opened my eyes and found that I
had been deluded. And despite my having called out that name, my
voice was so broken by my sobbing and weeping that those women
could not understand me, it seemed to me; and even though I was
greatly ashamed, nevertheless by some admonition of Love I turned
toward them. And when they saw me, they started to say: "He looks
like a dead man," and to say to one another, "Let us try to console
him"; so that they spoke many comforting words to me, at times ask-
ing me what I had been afraid of. So that I, being a little comforted,
and recognizing the falsity of my imaginings, answered them: "I will
tell you what troubled me." Then, all the way from the beginning to
the end, I told them what I had seen, only omitting the name of that
most noble lady. And so, afterward, having recovered from that ail-
ment, I resolved to write a poem about what had befallen me, because
I thought it was a lovable thing to hear; and so I wrote this ode about
it: "A compassionate lady of tender years," arranged as the division
below will make clear.

> A compassionate lady of tender years,
>   largely adorned with humane kindness,
>   who was present when I frequently called on Death,
>   seeing my eyes full of pity,
>   and hearing my rambling words,
>   took fright and began to weep heavily.
>   And other women who had taken notice
>   of me because that one was weeping with me,
>   made her depart,

e appressarsi per farmi sentire.
Qual dicea: «Non dormire»,
e qual dicea: «Perchè sì ti sconforte?».
Allor lassai la nova fantasia,
chiamando il nome de la donna mia.
Era la voce mia sì dolorosa
e rotta sì da l'angoscia del pianto,
ch'io solo intesi il nome nel mio core;
e con tutta la vista vergognosa
ch'era nel viso mio giunta cotanto,
mi fece verso lor volgere Amore.
Elli era tale a veder mio colore,
che facea ragionar di morte altrui:
«Deh, consoliam costui»
pregava l'una l'altra umilemente;
e dicevan sovente:
«Che vedestù, che tu non hai valore?».
E quando un poco confortato fui,
io dissi: «Donne, dicerollo a vui.
Mentr'io pensava la mia frale vita,
e vedea 'l suo durar com'è leggiero,
piansemi Amor nel core, ove dimora;
per che l'anima mia fu sì smarrita,
che sospirando dicea nel pensero:
—Ben converrà che la mia donna mora.—
Io presi tanto smarrimento allora,
ch'io chiusi li occhi vilmente gravati,
e furon sì smagati
li spirti miei, che ciascun giva errando;
e poscia imaginando,
di caunoscenza e di verità fora,
visi di donne m'apparver crucciati,
che mi dicean pur: —Morra'ti, morra'ti.—
Poi vidi cose dubitose molto,
nel vano imaginare ov'io entrai;
ed esser mi parea non so in qual loco,
e veder donne andar per via disciolte,
qual lagrimando, e qual traendo guai,
che di tristizia saettavan foco.
Poi mi parve vedere a poco a poco
turbar lo sole e apparir la stella,

and approached to bring me to my senses.
One said, "Do not sleep,"
and another said, "Why are you so dismayed?"
Then I abandoned those odd fancies,
calling out my lady's name.
My voice was so sorrowful
and so broken by the anguish of my weeping,
that I heard the name only in my heart;
and with the entire expression of shame
that had so overspread my face,
Love made me turn toward them.
My coloring was such to see
that it made someone speak of death:
"Come, let us comfort him,"
one woman urged the other humbly;
and they frequently said:
"What did you see to weaken you so?"
And when I was somewhat comforted,
I said: "Ladies, I shall tell you.
While I was pondering the debility of my life,
and realizing how brief its duration is,
Love wept in my heart, where he resides;
and thus my soul was so confused
that it said, with a sigh, in my mind:
'Of necessity my lady must surely die.'
Then I became so confused
that I shut my eyes, which were heavy with cowardice,
and my spirits
were so bewildered that each one went astray;
and then in my imagination,
far from awareness and from truth,
I thought I saw angry women's faces,
constantly saying to me: 'You will die, you will die.'
Then I saw very frightening things
in the empty ramblings of my mind;
and I thought I was I know not where,
seeing disheveled women walk down the street,
some weeping, others wailing,
and all darting flames of sorrow.
Then I thought I saw gradually
the sun darkened and the stars coming out,

e pianger elli ed ella;
cader li augelli volando per l'are,
e la terra tremare;
ed omo apparve scolorito e fioco,
dicendomi: —Che fai? non sai novella?
morta è la donna tua, ch'era sì bella.—
Levava li occhi miei bagnati in pianti,
e vedea, che parean pioggia di manna,
li angeli che tornavan suso in cielo,
e una nuvoletta avean davanti,
dopo la qual gridavan tutti: *Osanna;*
e s'altro avesser detto, a voi dire'lo.
Allor diceva Amor: —Più nol ti celo;
vieni a veder nostra donna che giace.—
Lo imaginar fallace
mi condusse a veder madonna morta;
e quand'io l'avea scorta,
vedea che donne la covrian d'un velo;
ed avea seco umilità verace,
che parea che dicesse: —Io sono in pace.—
Io divenia nel dolor sì umile,
veggendo in lei tanta umiltà formata,
ch'io dicea: —Morte, assai dolce ti tegno;
tu dei omai esser cosa gentile,
poi che tu se'ne la mia donna stata,
e dei aver pietate e non disdegno.
Vedi che sì desideroso vegno
d'esser de'tuoi, ch'io ti somiglio in fede.
Vieni, chè 'l cor te chiede.—
Poi mi partia, consumato ogne duolo;
e quand'io era solo,
dicea, guardando verso l'alto regno:
—Beato, anima bella, chi te vede!—
Voi mi chiamaste allor, vostra merzede.

Questa canzone ha due parti: ne la prima dico, parlando a indiffinita persona, come io fui levato d'una vana fantasia da certe donne, e come promisi loro di dirla; ne la seconda dico come io dissi a loro. La seconda comincia quivi: *Mentr'io pensava.* La prima parte si divide in due: ne la prima dico quello che certe donne, e che una sola, dissero e fecero per la mia fantasia quanto è dinanzi che io fossi tornato in ve-

and both sun and stars weeping;
  the birds that flew through the air falling,
  and the earth shaking;
  and a pale, hoarse man appeared,
  telling me: 'What are you doing? Have you not heard the news?
  Your lady, who was so beautiful, is dead.'
I raised my eyes wet with tears,
  and I saw, resembling a rain of manna,
  the angels going back up to heaven,
  and they had a little cloud in front of them,
  behind which they were all crying 'Hosanna';
  if they had said any more, I would tell you.
  Then Love said: 'I conceal it from you no longer;
  come to see our lady lying dead.'
  The false vision
  led me to see my lady dead;
  and when I had discerned her,
  I saw women covering her with a veil;
  and she had true humility with her,
  so that she seemed to say: 'I am in peace.'
In my sorrow I became so humble,
  seeing such great humility taking shape in her,
  that I said: 'Death, very sweet I deem you;
  by now you must be a kindly thing,
  because you have been in my lady,
  and you must feel pity and not disdain.
  You see that I am coming so desirous
  of being one of yours that I honestly resemble you.
  Come, for my heart requests you.'
  Then I departed, all sorrow consumed;
  and when I was alone,
  I said, looking up at the lofty realm:
  'Blessed, beautiful soul, is he who sees you!'
  Then you ladies called to me, for which I thank you."

  This ode has two parts: in the first, addressing an unspecified person,
I tell how I was rescued from an empty imagining by certain women, and
how I promised them to recount it; in the second, I recount what I told
them. The second begins with the words "'While I was pondering.'" The
first part is subdivided in two: in the first part, I report what certain
women, and what a single woman, said and did for my imaginings before

race condizione; ne la seconda dico quello che queste donne mi dissero poi che io lasciai questo farneticare; e comincia questa parte quivi: *Era la voce mia.* Poscia quando dico: *Mentr'io pensava,* dico come io dissi loro questa mia imaginazione. Ed intorno a ciò foe due parti: ne la prima dico per ordine questa imaginazione; ne la seconda, dicendo a che ora mi chiamaro, le ringrazio chiusamente; e comincia quivi questa parte: *Voi mi chiamaste.*

XXIV. Appresso questa vana imaginazione, avvenne uno die che, sedendo io pensoso in alcuna parte, ed io mi sentio cominciare un tremuoto nel cuore, così come se io fosse stato presente a questa donna. Allora dico che mi giunse una imaginazione d'Amore; che mi parve vederlo venire da quella parte ove la mia donna stava, e pareami che lietamente mi dicesse nel cor mio: «Pensa di benedicere lo dì che io ti presi, però che tu lo dei fare». E certo me parea avere lo cuore sì lieto, che me non parea che fosse lo mio cuore, per la sua nuova condizione. E poco dopo queste parole, che lo cuore mi disse con la lingua d'Amore, io vidi venire verso me una gentile donna, la quale era di famosa bieltade, e fue già molto donna di questo primo mio amico. E lo nome di questa donna era Giovanna, salvo che per la sua bieltade, secondo che altri crede, imposto l'era nome Primavera; e così era chiamata. E appresso lei, guardando, vidi venire la mirabile Beatrice. Queste donne andaro presso di me così l'una appresso l'altra, e parve che Amore mi parlasse nel cuore, e dicesse: «Quella prima è nominata Primavera solo per questa venuta d'oggi; chè io mossi lo imponitore del nome a chiamarla così Primavera, cioè prima verrà lo die che Beatrice si mosterrà dopo la imaginazione del suo fedele. E se anche vogli considerare lo primo nome suo, tanto è quanto dire —prima verrà,— però che lo suo nome Giovanna è da quello Giovanni lo quale precedette la verace luce, dicendo: —Ego vox clamantis in deserto: parate viam Domini.— Ed anche mi parve che mi dicesse, dopo, queste parole: «E chi volesse sottilmente considerare, quella Beatrice chiamerebbe Amore, per molta simiglianza che ha meco». Onde io poi, ripensando, propuosi di scrivere per rima a lo mio primo amico (tacendomi certe parole le quali pareano da tacere), credendo io che ancor lo suo cuore mirasse la bieltade di questa Primavera gentile; e dissi questo sonetto, lo quale comincia: *Io mi senti'svegliar.*

> Io mi senti'svegliar dentro a lo core
>   un spirito amoroso che dormia:
>   e poi vidi venir da lungi Amore

I had recovered my normal state of mind; in the second, I report what those women said to me after I had left off that mad behavior; and that part begins with "My voice was." When I later say "'While I was pondering,'" I relate how I recounted those fantasies of mine to them. And concerning this I make two parts: in the first, I narrate those fantasies in sequence; in the second, telling at what time they called me, I thank them in conclusion; and this part begins with the words "Then you ladies."

XXIV. After those idle fancies, it befell one day that, while I was sitting somewhere pensively, I felt a trembling begin in my heart, as if I had been in that lady's presence. Then (I say) a vision of Love came to me; I thought I saw him coming from where my lady was, and I thought he joyfully said in my heart: "Have a mind to bless the day when I took you captive, because you ought to." And indeed I thought my heart was so joyous that I could not believe it was my own heart, it had changed so. And shortly after those words, which my heart spoke to me with the tongue of Love, I saw approaching me a gentlewoman who was famous for her beauty, and who long before had been the sweetheart of that foremost friend of mine. And the name of that lady was Giovanna, although for her beauty, as people believe, she had been dubbed Primavera—Springtime—and she went by that name. And after her, as I looked, I saw the wondrous Beatrice coming. Those ladies approached me that way, one after the other, and Love seemed to be addressing me in my heart, saying: "That first one is named Primavera solely because of her arrival here today; for I induced the man who so dubbed her to call her Primavera because she will come first—*prima verrà*—on the day Beatrice shows herself after her devotee's fantasies. And if you wish to think about her earlier name as well, it, too, signifies 'she will come first,' because that name Giovanna comes from the Giovanni—Saint John the Baptist—who preceded the True Light, saying: 'I am the voice of one crying in the wilderness, Prepare ye the way of the Lord.'"[15] And I also thought he then said these words to me: "If you troubled to think about it carefully, that lady Beatrice would be called Love, for her great resemblance to me." So that, later, thinking this over, I resolved to write in verse to my foremost friend (omitting certain words that it seemed proper to omit), believing that his heart was still admiring the beauty of that noble Primavera; and I wrote this sonnet, which begins: "I felt awakening."

> I felt awakening within my heart
>   a loving spirit that was asleep;
>   and then I saw Love coming from afar

15. Compare Matthew 3:3.

allegro sì, che appena il conoscia,
dicendo: «Or pensa pur di farmi onore»;
e 'n ciascuna parola sua ridia.
E poco stando meco il mio segnore,
guardando in quella parte onde venia,
io vidi monna Vanna e monna Bice
venire inver lo loco là 'v'io era,
l'una appresso de l'altra maraviglia;
e sì come la mente mi ridice,
Amor mi disse: «Quell'è Primavera,
e quell'ha nome Amor, sì mi somiglia».

Questo sonetto ha molte parti: la prima delle quali dice come io mi
senti'svegliare lo tremore usato nel cuore, e come parve che Amore
m'apparisse allegro nel mio cuore da lunga parte; la seconda dice
come me parea che Amore mi dicesse nel mio cuore, e quale mi
parea; la terza dice come, poi che questi fue alquanto stato meco co-
tale, io vidi e udio certe cose. La seconda parte comincia quivi: *di-
cendo: Or pensa;* la terza quivi: *E poco stando.* La terza parte si divide
in due: ne la prima dico quello che io vidi; ne la seconda dico quello
che io udio. La seconda comincia quivi: *Amor mi disse.*

XXV. Potrebbe qui dubitare persona degna da dichiararle onne
dubitazione, e dubitare potrebbe di ciò, che io dico d'Amore come
se fosse una cosa per sè, e non solamente sustanzia intelligente, ma
sì come fosse sustanzia corporale: la quale cosa, secondo la veritate,
è falsa; chè Amore non è per sè sì come sustanzia, ma è uno acci-
dente in sustanzia. E che io dica di lui come se fosse corpo, ancora
sì come se fosse uomo, appare per tre cose che dico di lui. Dico che
lo vidi venire; onde, con ciò sia cosa che venire dica moto locale, e
localmente mobile per sè, secondo lo Filosofo, sia solamente corpo,
appare che io ponga Amore essere corpo. Dico anche di lui che
ridea, e anche che parlava; le quali cose paiono essere proprie de
l'uomo, e spezialmente essere risibile; e però appare ch'io ponga lui
essere uomo. A cotale cosa dichiarare, secondo che è buono a pre-
sente, prima è da intendere che anticamente non erano dicitori
d'amore in lingua volgare, anzi erano dicitori d'amore certi poete in
lingua latina; tra noi, dico, avvegna forse che tra altra gente addi-
venisse, e addivegna ancora, sì come in Grecia, non volgari ma lit-
terati poete queste cose trattavano. E non è molto numero d'anni
passati, che appariro prima questi poete volgari; chè dire per rima in

so cheerfully that I hardly knew him,
and saying: "Now make it your business to honor me";
and with every word of his he laughed.
And after my master had been with me a short while,
when I looked in the direction he had come from,
I saw Lady Vanna and Lady Bice
coming toward the place where I stood,
one marvel after the other;
and as my memory recalls to me,
Love said to me: "That one is Springtime,
and that one is called Love, she so resembles me."

This sonnet has many parts, the first of which tells how I felt the cus-
tomary trembling awaken in my heart, and how Love seemed to appear
joyously in my heart from far away; the second tells how I thought Love
was addressing me in my heart, and what he looked like; the third tells
how, after he had been with me that way for a while, I saw and heard
certain things. The second part begins with the words "and saying, 'Now
make it'"; the third, with "And after my master." The third part is sub-
divided in two: in the first part I tell what I saw; in the second, I tell
what I heard. This second subdivision begins with "Love said to me."

XXV. At this point, people deserving of having all dubious points ex-
plained to them might well hesitate, and might do so because I speak of
Love as if it were a thing in itself, and not merely a mental construct, but
as if it were a bodily substance: in strict truth, this is erroneous, for Love is
not like a substance in itself, but is an accident, a nonessential aspect, of
substance. And that I speak of it as if it were corporeal, and even as if it
were a man, is evident from three things that I say of it, or "him." I say I
saw him coming; so that, inasmuch as coming indicates movement in
space and, according to the Philosopher,[16] only bodies can perform move-
ment in space, I am evidently positing Love to be corporeal. I also say of
him that he was laughing, and also that he was speaking, things which
seem to be peculiar to man, especially the ability to laugh; and thus I evi-
dently posit him to be human. To explain such things, to the extent that is
suitable at present, I must first remind my readers that in olden times
there were no minstrels of love in the vernacular; rather, only certain poets
writing in Latin treated of love; in *our* land, I say, though perhaps the same
thing occurred, and may still occur, among other nations, just as in Greece
these matters were handled not by vernacular poets but by those writing
in the literary language. And it is not many years ago that such vernacular

---

16. Aristotle.

volgare tanto è quanto dire per versi in latino, secondo alcuna pro-
porzione. E segno che sia picciolo tempo, è che se volemo cercare
in lingua d'*oco* e in quella di *sì*, noi non troviamo cose dette anzi lo
presente tempo per cento e cinquanta anni. E la cagione per che al-
quanti grossi ebbero fama di sapere dire, è che quasi fuoro li primi
che dissero in lingua di *sì*. E lo primo che cominciò a dire sì come
poeta volgare, si mosse però che volle fare intendere le sue parole a
donna, a la quale era malagevole d'intendere li versi latini. E questo
è contra coloro che rimano sopra altra matera che amorosa, con ciò
sia cosa che cotale modo di parlare fosse dal principio trovato per
dire d'amore. Onde, con ciò sia cosa che a li poete sia conceduta
maggiore licenza di parlare che a li prosaici dittatori, e questi dici-
tori per rima non siano altro che poete volgari, degno e ragionevole
è che a loro sia maggiore licenzia largita di parlare che a li altri par-
latori volgari: onde, se alcuna figura o colore rettorico è conceduto a
li poete, conceduto è a li rimatori. Dunque, se noi vedemo che li
poete hanno parlato a le cose inanimate, sì come se avessero senso e
ragione, e fattele parlare insieme; e non solamente cose vere, ma
cose non vere, cioè che detto hanno, di cose le quali non sono, che
parlano, e detto che molti accidenti parlano, sì come se fossero su-
stanzie e uomini; degno è lo dicitore per rima di fare lo somigliante,
ma non sanza ragione alcuna, ma con ragione la quale poi sia possi-
bile d'aprire per prosa. Che li poete abbiano così parlato come detto
è, appare per Virgilio; lo quale dice che Iuno, cioè una dea nemica
de li Troiani, parloe ad Eolo, segnore de li venti, quivi nel primo de
lo Eneida: *Eole, nanque tibi,* e che questo segnore le rispuose, quivi:
*Tuus, o regina, quid optes explorare labor; michi iussa capessere fas
est.* Per questo medesimo poeta parla la cosa che non è animata a le
cose animate, nel terzo de lo Eneida, quivi: *Dardanide duri.* Per Lu-
cano parla la cosa animata a la cosa inanimata, quivi: *Multum, Roma,
tamen debes civilibus armis.* Per Orazio parla l'uomo a la scienzia
medesima sì come ad altra persona; e non solamente sono parole
d'Orazio, ma dicele quasi recitando lo modo del buono Omero, quivi
ne la sua Poetria: *Dic michi, Musa, virum.* Per Ovidio parla Amore,
sì come se fosse persona umana, ne lo principio de lo libro c'ha
nome Libro di Remedio d'Amore, quivi: *Bella michi, video, bella
parantur, ait.* E per questo puote essere manifesto a chi dubita in al-
cuna parte di questo mio libello. E acciò che non ne pigli alcuna bal-

poets first appeared among us; for to compose vernacular rhyming verse is tantamount, in some measure, to writing Latin metrical poetry. And it is a sign of the little time elapsed that, if we search through writings in Provençal and Italian, we do not find material earlier than a hundred fifty years before the present day. And the reason why a few unrefined men gained a reputation for skill in poetry is that they were practically the first to write verse in Italian. And the first man who began writing as a vernacular poet was induced to do so because he wanted his words to be understood by a lady, for whom Latin metrical verse was hard to understand. And this stands in opposition to those who rhyme on any other subject but love, inasmuch as this mode of utterance was originally devised to speak of love. So that, inasmuch as poets are granted greater license of speech than authors of prose, and these writers in rhyme, and vernacular poets, are one and the same thing, it is fitting and reasonable that they be granted greater license of utterance than the other vernacular speakers: hence, if any imagery or rhetorical figure is allowed to the Latin metrical poets, it is allowed to the rhymesters. Therefore, if we observe that the metrical poets have addressed inanimate objects as if they had sense and reason, and have made them address one another, and not only real things but also unreal things; that is, if we observe that they have said that nonexistent things speak and have said that many accidental aspects of things speak, as if they were substances and human beings, the vernacular poet is deserving of doing similar things, but not without some underlying reasoning: there must be a logic which it is later possible to expound in prose. That the metrical poets spoke as I have said is evident from Virgil, who states that Juno, who was a goddess hostile to the Trojans, spoke to Aeolus, master of the winds, in the first book of the *Aeneid*, "Aeolus, for to you . . . ,"[17] and that that lord answered her, "O queen, yours be the effort to determine what you wish; my duty is to carry out orders."[18] In this same poet, an inanimate thing addresses animate things in the third book of the *Aeneid*: "Harsh descendants of Dardanus."[19] In Lucan, an animate thing addresses an inanimate one: "And yet, Rome, you owe a lot to civil strife."[20] In Horace, a man addresses knowledge itself as if it were another person; and these are not merely words of Horace, but he states them in his *Art of Poetry* as a quotation from good Homer: "Tell me, Muse, of the man."[21] In Ovid, Love speaks as if it were a human being at the beginning of the book called *The Remedy for Love*: "Wars, I see, wars are being prepared against me,' he said."[22] And thereby it may be clear to anyone who hesitates over any

---

17. *Aeneid* I, 65.   18. I, 76–77.   19. III, 94.   20. *Pharsalia* I, 44.   21. *Ars poetica*, 141 (compare *Odyssey* I, 1).   22. *De remedio amoris* I, 2.

danza persona grossa, dico che nè li poete parlavano così sanza ra-
gione, nè quelli che rimano deono parlare così non avendo alcuno
ragionamento in loro di quello che dicono; però che grande ver-
gogna sarebbe a colui che rimasse cose sotto vesta di figura o di co-
lore rettorico, e poscia, domandato, non sapesse denudare le sue
parole da cotale vesta, in guisa che avessero verace intendimento. E
questo mio primo amico e io ne sapemo bene di quelli che così ri-
mano stoltamente.

XXVI. Questa gentilissima donna, di cui ragionato è ne le prece-
denti parole, venne in tanta grazia de le genti, che quando passava per
via, le persone correano per vedere lei; onde mirabile letizia me ne
giungea. E quando ella fosse presso d'alcuno, tanta onestade giungea
nel cuore di quello, che non ardia di levare li occhi, nè di rispondere
a lo suo saluto; e di questo molti, sì come esperti, mi potrebbero te-
stimoniare a chi non lo credesse. Ella coronata e vestita d'umilitade
s'andava, nulla gloria mostrando di ciò ch'ella vedea e udia. Diceano
molti, poi che passata era: «Questa non è femmina, anzi è uno de li
bellissimi angeli del cielo». E altri diceano: «Questa è una maraviglia;
che benedetto sia lo Segnore, che sì mirabilmente sae adoperare!».
Io dico ch'ella si mostrava sì gentile e sì piena di tutti li piaceri, che
quelli che la miravano comprendeano in loro una dolcezza onesta e
soave, tanto che ridicere non lo sapeano; nè alcuno era lo quale
potesse mirare lei, che nel principio nol convenisse sospirare. Queste
e più mirabili cose da lei procedeano virtuosamente: onde io pen-
sando a ciò, volendo ripigliare lo stilo de la sua loda, proposi di dicere
parole, ne le quali io dessi ad intendere de le sue mirabili ed eccellenti
operazioni; acciò che non pur coloro che la poteano sensibilmente
vedere, ma li altri sappiano di lei quello che le parole ne possono fare
intendere. Allora dissi questo sonetto, lo quale comincia: *Tanto gen-
tile*.

> Tanto gentile e tanto onesta pare
>   la donna mia quand'ella altrui saluta,
>   ch'ogne lingua deven tremando muta,
>   e li occhi no l'ardiscon di guardare.
>   Ella si va, sentendosi laudare,
>   benignamente d'umiltà vestuta;
>   e par che sia una cosa venuta
>   da cielo in terra a miracol mostrare.
> Mostrasi sì piacente a chi la mira,
>   che dà per li occhi una dolcezza al core,

part of this little book of mine. And so that no unrefined person may be emboldened by this, I state that the old metrical poets never spoke this way without a reason, nor should the rhymesters of today speak this way without some underlying logic in what they are saying; because it would be very shameful for a man who wrote poems using imagery and rhetorical figures if he were later asked and was unable to divest his words of that garb so that their true meaning was clear. And that foremost friend of mine is as well acquainted as I am with people who write such foolish verse.

XXVI. That most noble lady who has been mentioned in the foregoing text, fell into such great favor with the people that, when she walked down the street, they would run up to look at her; this caused me wondrous joy. And when she was near anyone, so much modesty filled his heart that he did not dare to raise his eyes or answer her greeting; and many could testify to this, as having experienced it, if anyone failed to believe it. She went about crowned and clad in humility, showing no false pride in what she saw and heard. Many used to say, after she had gone by: "She is not a woman, she is one of the very beautiful angels in heaven." And others said: "She is a wonder; blessed be the Lord, who is able to perform such miracles!" I assert that she showed herself to be so noble and so filled with all delights that those who beheld her felt within themselves such a modest and gentle sweetness that they were unable to express it; nor was there anyone who could behold her without being compelled at first to sigh. These and more remarkable things emanated from her virtue: and so, with that in mind, and wishing to grasp my stylus again in praise of her, I resolved to write a poem in which I could communicate some of her wondrous and excellent influences, so that not only those who were able to see her with their own eyes, but others as well, might know of her as much as words can communicate. Then I wrote this sonnet, which begins: "So noble."

So noble and so modest appears
    my lady when she greets others,
    that every tongue trembles and becomes mute,
    and their eyes do not dare to look at her.
She passes by, hearing herself praised,
    benignly clad in humility;
    and she seems to be something that has descended
    from heaven to earth to manifest a miracle.
She appears so delightful to those who behold her
    that, through the eyes, she gives to the heart a sweetness

> che 'ntender no la può chi no la prova:
> e par che de la sua labbia si mova
> un spirito soave pien d'amore,
> che va dicendo a l'anima: Sospira.

Questo sonetto è sì piano ad intendere, per quello che narrato è di-
nanzi, che non abbisogna d'alcuna divisione; e però lassando lui, dico
che questa mia donna venne in tanta grazia, che non solamente ella
era onorata e laudata, ma per lei erano onorate e laudate molte. On-
d'io, veggendo ciò e volendo manifestare a chi ciò non vedea, propuo-
si anche di dire parole, ne le quali ciò fosse significato; e dissi allora
questo altro sonetto, che comincia: *Vede perfettamente onne salute,* lo
quale narra di lei come la sua vertude adoperava ne l'altre, sì come ap-
pare ne la sua divisione.

> Vede perfettamente onne salute
> chi la mia donna tra le donne vede;
> quelle che vanno con lei son tenute
> di bella grazia a Dio render merzede.
> E sua bieltate è di tanta vertute,
> che nulla invidia a l'altre ne procede,
> anzi le face andar seco vestute
> di gentilezza, d'amore e di fede.
> La vista sua fa onne cosa umile;
> e non fa sola sè parer piacente,
> ma ciascuna per lei riceve onore.
> Ed è ne li atti suoi tanto gentile,
> che nessun la si può recare a mente,
> che non sospiri in dolcezza d'amore.

Questo sonetto ha tre parti: ne la prima dico tra che gente questa
donna più mirabile parea; ne la seconda dico sì come era graziosa la
sua compagnia; ne la terza dico di quelle cose che vertuosamente
operava in altrui. La seconda parte comincia quivi: *quelle che vanno;*
la terza quivi: *E sua bieltate.* Questa ultima parte si divide in tre: ne la
prima dico quello che operava ne le donne, cioè per loro medesime;
ne la seconda dico quello che operava in loro per altrui; ne la terza
dico come non solamente ne le donne, ma in tutte le persone, e non
solamente ne la sua presenzia, ma ricordandosi di lei, mirabilmente
operava. La seconda comincia quivi: *La vista sua;* la terza quivi: *Ed è
ne li atti.*

XXVII. Appresso ciò, cominciai a pensare uno giorno sopra quello

which no one can understand who does not experience it;
and there seems to issue from her lips
a gentle spirit full of love
that keeps telling the soul: "Sigh!"

This sonnet is so easy to understand, through what was narrated before, that it needs no analysis; and so, moving onward, I state that this lady of mine fell into such great favor that not only was she honored and praised, but also many other women were honored and praised on her account. Wherefore, seeing this and wishing to make it clear to those who did not see it, I resolved to write another poem in which it would be declared; and I then wrote this other sonnet, beginning "He sees all salvation perfectly," which tells of how her virtue influenced other women, as will be clear when I analyze it.

He sees all salvation perfectly
    who sees my lady among other women;
    those women who go with her are obliged
    to thank God for such a fine favor.
    And her beauty is of such an effect
    that it produces no envy in other women;
    rather, it makes them go with her clad
    in nobility, love, and faith.
The sight of her makes everything humble;
    and not only makes *her* appear pleasant,
    but also makes every woman receive honor on her account.
    And she is so noble in her actions
    that no one can recall her to mind
    and fail to sigh in the sweetness of love.

This sonnet has three parts: in the first, I say among what people this lady appeared most wonderful; in the second, I tell how charming her company was; in the third, I speak of those things she effected in others through her virtuous powers. The second part begins with the words "those women who go"; the third, with "And her beauty." This last part is subdivided in three: in the first, I tell her effects on women, in themselves; in the second, I tell her effects on them indirectly, through others; in the third I tell how she worked wonders not only in women but in all people, and not merely when she was present but also when she was remembered. The second begins with the words "The sight of her"; the third, with "And she is so noble."

XXVII. After that, I began one day to think about what I had said

che detto avea de la mia donna, cioè in questi due sonetti precedenti;
e veggendo nel mio pensero che io non avea detto di quello che al pre-
sente tempo adoperava in me, pareami defettivamente avere parlato.
E però propuosi di dire parole, ne le quali io dicesse come me parea
essere disposto a la sua operazione, e come operava in me la sua ver-
tude; e non credendo potere ciò narrare in brevitade di sonetto, co-
minciai allora una canzone, la quale comincia: *Sì lungiamente*.

> Sì lungiamente m'ha tenuto Amore
> e costumato a la sua segnoria,
> che sì com'elli m'era forte in pria,
> così mi sta soave ora nel core.
> Però quando mi tolle sì 'l valore,
> che li spiriti par che fuggan via,
> allor sente la frale anima mia
> tanta dolcezza, che 'l viso ne smore,
> poi prende Amore in me tanta vertute,
> che fa li miei spiriti gir parlando,
> ed escon for chiamando
> la donna mia, per darmi più salute.
> Questo m'avvene ovunque ella mi vede,
> e sì è cosa umil, che nol si crede.

XXVIII. *Quomodo sedet sola civitas plena populo! facta est quasi
vidua domina gentium.* Io era nel proponimento ancora di questa can-
zone, e compiuta n'avea questa soprascritta stanzia, quando lo segnore
de la giustizia chiamoe questa gentilissima a gloriare sotto la insegna
di quella regina benedetta virgo Maria, lo cui nome fue in grandissima
reverenzia ne le parole di questa Beatrice beata. E avvegna che forse
piacerebbe a presente trattare alquanto de la sua partita da noi, non è
lo mio intendimento di trattarne qui per tre ragioni: la prima è che ciò
non è del presente proposito, se volemo guardare nel proemio che
precede questo libello; la seconda si è che, posto che fosse del pre-
sente proposito, ancora non sarebbe sufficiente la mia lingua a trattare
come si converrebbe di ciò; la terza si è che, posto che fosse l'uno e
l'altro, non è convenevole a me trattare di ciò, per quello che, trat-
tando, converrebbe essere me laudatore di me medesimo, la quale
cosa è al postutto biasimevole a chi lo fae; e però lascio cotale trattato
ad altro chiosatore. Tuttavia, però che molte volte lo numero del nove
ha preso luogo tra le parole dinanzi, onde pare che sia non sanza ra-

of my lady; that is, in those two foregoing sonnets; and finding in my
reflections that I had not spoken about her effect on me at that time,
I thought my utterance had been deficient. And so I resolved to write
a poem in which I would tell how open I felt I was to her influence,
and how her virtue affected me; and thinking I could not recount all
that in the short space of a sonnet, I then began an ode, which begins:
"So long."

> So long has Love held me
>   and accustomed me to his mastery
>   that, just as he was formerly harsh to me,
>   now he resides gently in my heart.
>   So, when he deprives me of strength so extremely
>   that my spirits seem to be fleeting away,
>   then my frail soul feels
>   such sweetness that my face grows pale;
>   then Love assumes so much power over me
>   that he makes my spirits go about speaking,
>   and they issue forth calling upon
>   my lady, to give me further salvation.
>   This befalls me wherever she sees me,
>   and it is something more delightful than can be believed.

XXVIII. "How doth the city sit solitary, that was full of people! how
is she become as a widow! she that was great among the nations."[23] I
was still planning that ode, and had completed that first stanza given
above, when the Lord of justice summoned that most noble lady to a
life of bliss under the banner of that blessed queen the Virgin Mary,
whose name was held in the greatest reverence in the speech of that
holy Beatrice. And although it might perhaps be pleasant right now to
say a little about her departure from us, I do not intend to do so here,
for three reasons: the first is that it is not to the present purpose, if we
take the trouble to recall the preamble that precedes this little book;
the second is that, even if it were to the present purpose, my tongue
would still be inadequate to treat of it fittingly; the third is that, even
if the first two reasons did not hold, it does not behoove me to treat
of this because, if I did, I would have to be a praiser of myself, which
after all is reprehensible in whoever does it; so that I leave that sub-
ject to another commentator. Nevertheless, because the number nine
has frequently found a place in my foregoing narrative, whence it ap-

---

23. Lamentations 1:1.

gione, e ne la sua partita cotale numero pare che avesse molto luogo, convenesi di dire quindi alcuna cosa, acciò che pare al proposito convenirsi. Onde prima dicerò come ebbe luogo ne la sua partita, e poi n'assegnerò alcuna ragione, per che questo numero fue a lei cotanto amico.

XXIX. Io dico che, secondo l'usanza d'Arabia, l'anima sua nobilissima si partio ne la prima ora del nono giorno del mese; e secondo l'usanza di Siria, ella si partio nel nono mese de l'anno, però che lo primo mese è ivi Tisirin primo, lo quale a noi è Ottobre; e secondo l'usanza nostra, ella si partio in quello anno de la nostra indizione, cioè de li anni Domini, in cui lo perfetto numero nove volte era compiuto in quello centinaio nel quale in questo mondo ella fue posta, ed ella fue de li cristiani del terzodecimo centinaio. Perchè questo numero fosse in tanto amico di lei, questa potrebbe essere una ragione: con ciò sia cosa che, secondo Tolomeo e secondo la cristiana veritade, nove siano li cieli che si muovono, e, secondo comune oppinione astrologa, li detti cieli adoperino qua giuso secondo la loro abitudine insieme, questo numero fue amico di lei per dare ad intendere che ne la sua generazione tutti e nove li mobili cieli perfettissimamente s'aveano insieme. Questa è una ragione di ciò; ma più sottilmente pensando, e secondo la infallibile veritade, questo numero fue ella medesima; per similitudine dico, e ciò intendo così. Lo numero del tre è la radice del nove, però che, sanza numero altro alcuno, per se medesimo fa nove, sì come vedemo manifestamente che tre via tre fa nove. Dunque se lo tre è fattore per se medesimo del nove, e lo fattore per se medesimo de li miracoli è tre, cioè Padre e Figlio e Spirito Santo, li quali sono tre e uno, questa donna fue accompagnata da questo numero del nove a dare ad intendere ch'ella era uno nove, cioè uno miracolo, la cui radice, cioè del miracolo, è solamente la mirabile Trinitade. Forse ancora per più sottile persona si vederebbe in ciò più sottile ragione; ma questa è quella ch'io ne veggio, e che più mi piace.

XXX. Poi che fue partita da questo secolo, rimase tutta la sopradetta cittade quasi vedova dispogliata da ogni dignitade; onde io, ancora lagrimando in questa desolata cittade, scrissi a li principi de la terra alquanto de la sua condizione, pigliando quello cominciamento di Geremia profeta che dice: *Quomodo sedet sola civitas*. E questo dico, acciò che altri non si maravigli perchè io l'abbia allegato di sopra, quasi come entrata de la nuova materia che appresso vene. E se al-

pears that this is not without some foundation, and since that number seems to have played a large part in her decease, it is therefore fitting to say something about it, seeming, as it does, to suit our purpose. So that I shall first tell how it played a part in her decease, and then I shall suggest some reason why that number was so congenial to her.

XXIX. I say that, according to the Arabian custom,[24] her very noble soul departed in the first hour of the ninth day of the month; and according to Syrian reckoning, she departed in the ninth month of the year, because the first month there is the first Tishri, which is our October; and according to our reckoning, she departed in that year of our calendar (that is, that *annus Domini*) in which the "perfect number" ten had been completed nine times in the century in which she had been born into this life (and she lived in the thirteenth Christian century). This may be a reason why that number was so congenial to her: inasmuch as, according to Ptolemy and Christian truth, there are nine moving heavens and, according to received astrological wisdom, those heavens affect us here below in proportion to their workings among themselves, that number was congenial to her to make us understand that at her conception all nine moving heavens were in perfect relation to one another. This is one reason for it; but, pondering it more subtly, and in accordance with infallible truth, she was herself that number, I mean by similitude, and here is what I have in mind. The number three is the square root of nine, because, without the intervention of any other number, it creates nine by itself, as we clearly see that three times three are nine. Therefore, if three in itself is the factor of nine, and the factor (or producer) of miracles is itself also three—that is, Father, Son, and Holy Spirit, who are three and one—that lady was accompanied by the number nine to make us understand that she was a nine (that is, a miracle), whose root (that is, the miracle's) is none other than the wondrous Trinity. Perhaps an even more profound thinker could find a more profound reason for this; but this is the one that I see, and which most pleases me.

XXX. After she departed from this life, all of the aforesaid city was left, as it were, a widow bereft of all dignity; so that I, still weeping in that desolate city, wrote to the princes of the land something of its condition, quoting those opening lines of the prophet Jeremiah which say: "How doth the city sit solitary." And I say this so that no one will be surprised at my having quoted it above, as if the opening of the new subject matter to follow. And if anyone should wish to blame me for not having set

---

24. In which a new day begins at nightfall.

cuno volesse me riprendere di ciò, ch'io non scrivo qui le parole che
seguitano a quelle allegate, escusomene, però che lo intendimento
mio non fue dal principio di scrivere altro che per volgare; onde, con
ciò sia cosa che le parole che seguitano a quelle che sono allegate,
siano tutte latine, sarebbe fuori del mio intendimento se le scrivessi.
E simile intenzione so ch'ebbe questo mio primo amico a cui io ciò
scrivo, cioè ch'io li scrivessi solamente volgare.

XXXI. Poi che li miei occhi ebbero per alquanto tempo lagrimato,
e tanto affaticati erano che non poteano disfogare la mia tristizia, pen-
sai di volere disfogarla con alquante parole dolorose; e però propuosi
di fare una canzone, ne la quale piangendo ragionassi di lei per cui
tanto dolore era fatto distruggitore de l'anima mia; e cominciai allora
una canzone, la qual comincia: *Li occhi dolenti per pietà del core*. E
acciò che questa canzone paia rimanere più vedova dopo lo suo fine,
la dividerò prima che io la scriva; e cotale modo terrò da qui innanzi.

Io dico che questa cattivella canzone ha tre parti: la prima è
proemio; ne la seconda ragiono di lei; ne la terza parlo a la canzone
pietosamente. La seconda parte comincia quivi: *Ita n'è Beatrice;* la
terza quivi: *Pietosa mia canzone*. La prima parte si divide in tre: ne la
prima dico perchè io mi muovo a dire; ne la seconda dico a cui io
voglio dire; ne la terza dico di cui io voglio dire. La seconda comincia
quivi: *E perchè me ricorda;* la terza quivi: *e dicerò*. Poscia quando
dico: *Ita n'è Beatrice,* ragiono di lei; e intorno a ciò foe due parti:
prima dico la cagione per che tolta ne fue; appresso dico come altri si
piange de la sua partita, e comincia questa parte quivi: *Partissi de la
sua*. Questa parte si divide in tre: ne la prima dico chi non la piange;
ne la seconda dico chi la piange; ne la terza dico de la mia condizione.
La seconda comincia quivi: *ma ven tristizia e voglia;* la terza quivi:
Dannomi angoscia. Poscia quando dico: *Pietosa mia canzone,* parlo a
questa canzone, disignandole a quali donne se ne vada, e steasi con
loro.

> Li occhi dolenti per pietà del core
>   hanno di lagrimar sofferta pena,
>   sì che per vinti son remasi omai.
> Ora, s'i'voglio sfogar lo dolore,
>   che a poco a poco a la morte mi mena,
>   convenemi parlar traendo guai.
> E perchè me ricorda ch'io parlai
>   de la mia donna, mentre che vivia,
>   donne gentili, volentier con vui,

down here the words that follow the ones I quoted, my apology is that from the outset my intention here has been to write solely in the vernacular; so that, inasmuch as the words that follow the ones quoted are all in Latin, it would be contrary to my intention to set them down. And I know that that foremost friend, to whom I am writing this, had a similar intention; that is, that I should write to him solely in the vernacular.

XXXI. After my eyes had wept for some time, and were so weary that they could not relieve my sadness, I thought I might relieve it with some words of sorrow; and so I resolved to write an ode in which I would tearfully speak of her, on whose account such great grief had become the destroyer of my soul; and I then began an ode which begins: "My eyes, grieving through my heart's pity." And in order that this ode may be left more "widowed" after it is over, I shall analyze it before I set it down; and I shall adhere to that system from this point on.

To resume, this sorrowful ode has three parts: the first is a preamble; in the second, I speak about her; in the third, I address the ode piteously. The second part begins with the words "Beatrice has gone"; the third, with "My compassionate ode." The first part is subdivided in three: in the first, I tell why I am moved to speak; in the second, I tell to whom I wish to speak; in the third, I tell of whom I wish to speak. The second subdivision begins with the words "And because I recall"; the third, with "and I shall speak." Later, when I say "Beatrice has gone," I speak about her; and on that subject I make two parts; first I state the reason why she was taken from us; then I tell how people lament her decease, and this part begins with the words "It departed from her." This part is subdivided in three: in the first, I tell who does not weep for her; in the second, I tell who does weep for her; in the third, I state my own condition. The second begins with the words "but sadness comes, and the desire"; the third, with "My heavy sighs." Later, when I say "My compassionate ode," I address this ode, indicating to it to which women it is to go and then remain with them.

> My eyes, grieving through my heart's pity,
>   have suffered pain from weeping,
>   so that by now they have been overcome.
> Now, if I want to relieve my sorrow,
>   which is gradually leading me toward death,
>   I am forced to speak in lament.
> And because I recall that I spoke
>   about my lady, while she was alive,
>   gladly with you, noble ladies,

non voi parlare altrui,
se non a cor gentil che in donna sia;
e dicerò di lei piangendo, pui
che si n'è gita in ciel subitamente,
e ha lasciato Amor meco dolente.
Ita n'è Beatrice in l'alto cielo,
nel reame ove li angeli hanno pace,
e sta con loro, e voi, donne, ha lassate:
no la ci tolse qualità di gelo
nè di calore, come l'altre face,
ma solo fue sua gran benignitate;
chè luce de la sua umilitate
passò li cieli con tanta vertute,
che fè maravigliar l'etterno sire,
sì che dolce disire
lo giunse di chiamar tanta salute;
e fella di qua giù a sè venire,
perchè vedea ch'esta vita noiosa
non era degna di sì gentil cosa.
Partissi de la sua bella persona
piena di grazia l'anima gentile,
ed èssi gloriosa in loco degno.
Chi no la piange, quando ne ragiona,
core ha di pietra sì malvagio e vile,
ch'entrar no i puote spirito benegno.
Non è di cor villan sì alto ingegno,
che possa imaginar di lei alquanto,
e però no li ven di pianger doglia:
ma ven tristizia e voglia
di sospirare e di morir di pianto,
e d'onne consolar l'anima spoglia
chi vede nel pensero alcuna volta
quale ella fue, e com'ella n'è tolta.
Dannomi angoscia li sospiri forte,
quando 'l pensero ne la mente grave
mi reca quella che m'ha 'l cor diviso:
e spesse fiate pensando a la morte,
venemene un disio tanto soave,
che mi tramuta lo color nel viso.
E quando 'l maginar mi ven ben fiso,
giugnemi tanta pena d'ogne parte,

I do not wish to address any other
than a noble heart belonging to a lady;
and I shall speak of her tearfully, now
that she has suddenly gone to heaven,
leaving Love to grieve with me.
Beatrice has gone to heaven above,
to the realm where the angels enjoy peace,
and she resides with them, having deserted you, ladies:
she was not taken from us by a chill
or a fever, as other women are;
it was merely her great benignity;
for the light of her humility
pierced the heavens with such force
that it made the Lord Eternal marvel,
so that a sweet desire
came to him to summon such salvation;
and he caused her to come to him from here below,
because he saw that this life of troubles
was not worthy of something so noble.
It departed from her beautiful body,
that noble soul full of grace,
and is now in glory in a worthy place.
Whoever does not lament her when he speaks of her
has a heart of stone, so wicked and base,
that no kindly spirit can enter it.
No lowly heart has enough intelligence
to be able to have any notion of her,
and so no sorrow touches it to make it weep;
but sadness comes, and the desire
to sigh and die of weeping,
divesting the soul of every consolation,
to whoever sometimes sees in his mind
of what nature she was, and how she is taken from us.
My heavy sighs cause me anguish
when the thoughts in my burdened mind
recall to me the lady who has broken my heart:
and, when I frequently think of death,
so gentle a desire overcomes me
that it changes the color in my face.
And when my ideas are firmly fixed,
I receive so much pain from every side

ch'io mi riscuoto per dolor ch'i'sento;
e sì fatto divento,
che da le genti vergogna mi parte.
Poscia piangendo, sol nel mio lamento
chiamo Beatrice, e dico: «Or se'tu morta?»;
e mentre ch'io la chiamo, me conforta.
Pianger di doglia e sospirar d'angoscia
mi strugge 'l core ovunque sol mi trovo,
sì che ne 'ncrescerebbe a chi m'audesse:
e quale è stata la mia vita, poscia
che la mia donna andò nel secol novo,
lingua non è che dicer lo sapesse:
e però, donne mie, pur ch'io volesse,
non vi saprei io dir ben quel ch'io sono,
sì mi fa travagliar l'acerba vita;
la quale è sì 'nvilita,
che ogn'om par che mi dica: «Io t'abbandono»,
veggendo la mia labbia tramortita.
Ma qual ch'io sia la mia donna il si vede,
e io ne spero ancor da lei merzede.
Pietosa mia canzone, or va piangendo;
e ritruova le donne e le donzelle
a cui le tue sorelle
erano usate di portar letizia;
e tu, che se'figliuola di tristizia,
vatten disconsolata a star con elle.

XXXII. Poi che detta fue questa canzone, sì venne a me uno, lo
quale, secondo li gradi de l'amistade, è amico a me immediatamente
dopo lo primo; e questi fue tanto distretto di sanguinitade con questa
gloriosa, che nullo più presso l'era. E poi che fue meco a ragionare, mi
pregoe ch'io li dovessi dire alcuna cosa per una donna che s'era morta;
e simulava sue parole, acciò che paresse che dicesse d'un'altra, la
quale morta era certamente: onde io, accorgendomi che questi dicea
solamente per questa benedetta, sì li dissi di fare ciò che mi doman-
dava lo suo prego. Onde poi, pensando a ciò, propuosi di fare uno
sonetto, nel quale mi lamentasse alquanto, e di darlo a questo mio
amico, acciò che paresse che per lui l'avessi fatto; e dissi allora questo
sonetto, che comincia: *Venite a intender li sospiri miei.* Lo quale ha
due parti: ne la prima chiamo li fedeli d'Amore che m'intendano; ne
la seconda narro de la mia misera condizione. La seconda comincia
quivi: *li quai disconsolati.*

that I shake with the sorrow I feel;
and I reach such a state
that shame separates me from other people.
Then, weeping, alone in my lament
I call on Beatrice, saying, "Are you dead now?"
And as I call her, she consoles me.
Sorrowful tears and anguished sighs
consume my heart wherever I find myself alone,
so that it would give grief to whoever heard me:
and what my life has been like ever since
my lady went to her new existence,
there is no tongue able to tell:
and so, my ladies, even if I wished
I could not tell you rightly what has become of me,
bitter life torments me so;
my life has become so base
that I imagine everyone is saying, "I abandon you,"
when they see my pallid face.
But my lady sees what has become of me,
and I still hope for recompense from her.
My compassionate ode, now depart in tears,
and seek out the ladies and maidens
to whom your sister poems
used to bring joy;
and you, who are a daughter of sadness,
depart disconsolate to stay with them.

XXXII. After that ode was written, a man came to see me who, in the degrees of friendship, is my second best friend, right after that foremost one; and this man was so close a blood relation to that lady who is in glory that there was none closer. And after chatting with me, he asked me to write some poems in memory of a lady who had died; and he used feigned words, making it appear as if he meant some other lady, who had surely died; but I, realizing that he was speaking of no other than my blessed lady, promised to do what he requested of me. So that then, thinking about this, I resolved to write a sonnet in which I would lament a little, and to give it to that friend of mine as if I had written it to his specifications; and then I wrote this sonnet, which begins: "Come hear my sighs." It has two parts: in the first, I call upon the devotees of Love to listen to me; in the second, I recount my wretched state. The second begins with the words "they issue from me."

Venite a intender li sospiri miei,
  oi cor gentili, chè pietà 'l disia:
  li quai disconsolati vanno via,
  e s'e'non fosser, di dolor morrei;
  però che gli occhi mi sarebber rei,
  molte fiate più ch'io non vorria,
  lasso!, di pianger sì la donna mia,
  che sfogasser lo cor, piangendo lei.
Voi udirete lor chiamar sovente
  la mia donna gentil, che si n'è gita
  al secol degno de la sua vertute;
  e dispregiar talora questa vita
  in persona de l'anima dolente
  abbandonata de la sua salute.

XXXIII. Poi che detto ei questo sonetto, pensandomi chi questi era a cui lo intendea dare quasi come per lui fatto, vidi che povero mi parea lo servigio e nudo a così distretta persona di questa gloriosa. E però anzi ch'io li dessi questo soprascritto sonetto, sì dissi due stanzie d'una canzone, l'una per costui veracemente, e l'altra per me, avvegna che paia l'una e l'altra per una persona detta, a chi non guarda sottilmente; ma chi sottilmente le mira vede bene che diverse persone parlano, acciò che l'una non chiama sua donna costei, e l'altra sì, come appare manifestamente. Questa canzone e questo soprascritto sonetto li diedi, dicendo io lui che per lui solo fatto l'avea.

La canzone comincia: *Quantunque volte,* e ha due parti: ne l'una, cioè ne la prima stanzia, si lamenta questo mio caro e distretto a lei; ne la seconda mi lamento io, cioè ne l'altra stanzia, che comincia: *E'sì raccoglie ne li miei.* E così appare che in questa canzone si lamentano due persone, l'una de le quali si lamenta come frate, l'altra come servo.

Quantunque volte, lasso!, mi rimembra
  ch'io non debbo già mai
  veder la donna ond'io vo sì dolente,
  tanto dolore intorno 'l cor m'assembra
  la dolorosa mente,
  ch'io dico: «Anima mia, chè non ten vai?
  chè li tormenti che tu porterai
  nel secol, che t'è già tanto noioso,
  mi fan pensoso di paura forte».

Come hear my sighs,
   O noble hearts, for pity demands it:
   they issue from me despairingly,
   and were it not for them, I would die of grief;
   because my eyes would be cruel to me,
   many times more than I would like,
   alas! if they wept so hard for my lady
   that they would relieve my heart while I was lamenting her.
You will hear those sighs frequently calling on
   my noble lady, who has gone
   to a life worthy of her virtue,
   and at times contemning this life
   in the name of the grieving soul
   that has been deserted by its salvation.

XXXIII. After writing this sonnet, I thought about the quality of the friend to whom I intended to give it as if it were a work of his own, and I found that it seemed like a poor, naked favor for someone so closely related to that lady who is in glory. And so, before I gave him the aforesaid sonnet, I wrote two stanzas of an ode, one truly in his voice and the other in mine, though both would seem to be spoken by one person if you did not examine them too carefully; but if you do, you will see clearly that two different people are speaking, one of whom does not call the woman "my lady," whereas the other does, as is clearly evident. I gave him this ode and the aforesaid sonnet, telling him that I had composed it solely for his purposes.

The ode begins: "Every time." It has two parts: in one, which is the first stanza, this friend of mine and relative of hers laments; in the second I lament—that is, in the second stanza, which begins: "And there takes shelter in my." And thus it appears as if two people were lamenting in this ode, one of whom laments like a brother, the other like a devoted servant.

Every time, alas! that I recall
   that I am never again to
   see the lady for whom I grieve so,
   such great sorrow is gathered around my heart
   by my sorrowful mind
   that I say: "My soul, why do you not depart?
   For the torments you will undergo
   in this life, which is already so burdensome to you,
   make me think strongly of fear."

Ond'io chiamo la Morte,
come soave e dolce mio riposo;
e dico «Vieni a me» con tanto amore,
che sono astioso di chiunque more.
E'si raccoglie ne li miei sospiri
un sono di pietate,
che va chiamando Morte tuttavia:
a lei si volser tutti i miei disiri,
quando la donna mia
fu giunta da la sua crudelitate;
perchè 'l piacere de la sua bieltate,
partendo sè da la nostra veduta,
divenne spiritual bellezza grande,
che per lo cielo spande
luce d'amor, che li angeli saluta,
e lo intelletto loro alto, sottile
face maravigliar, sì v'è gentile.

XXXIV. In quello giorno nel quale si compiea l'anno che questa donna era fatta de li cittadini di vita eterna, io mi sedea in parte ne la quale, ricordandomi di lei, disegnava uno angelo sopra certe tavolette; e mentre io lo disegnava, volsi li occhi, e vidi lungo me uomini a li quali si convenia di fare onore. E'riguardavano quello che io facea; e secondo che me fu detto poi, elli erano stati già alquanto anzi che io me ne accorgesse. Quando li vidi, mi levai, e salutando loro dissi: «Altri era testè meco, però pensava». Onde partiti costoro, ritornaimi a la mia opera, cioè del disegnare figure d'angeli: e faccendo ciò, mi venne uno pensero di dire parole, quasi per annovale, e scrivere a costoro li quali erano venuti a me; e dissi allora questo sonetto, lo quale comincia: *Era venuta;* lo quale ha due cominciamenti, e però lo dividerò secondo l'uno e secondo l'altro.

Dico che secondo lo primo questo sonetto ha tre parti: ne la prima dico che questa donna era già ne la mia memoria; ne la seconda dico quello che Amore però mi facea; ne la terza dico de gli effetti d'Amore. La seconda comincia quivi: *Amor, che;* la terza quivi: *Piangendo uscivan for.* Questa parte si divide in due: ne l'una dico che tutti li miei sospiri uscivano parlando; ne la seconda dico che alquanti diceano certe parole diverse da gli altri. La seconda comincia quivi: *Ma quei.* Per questo medesimo modo si divide secondo l'altro cominciamento, salvo che ne la prima parte dico quando questa donna era così venuta ne la mia memoria, e ciò non dico ne l'altro.

So that I call upon Death
as a sweet, gentle repose for me,
and I say "Come to me" so lovingly
that I begrudge whoever dies.
And there takes shelter in my sighs
a sound of compassion
which constantly calls upon Death:
to it all my desires were directed
when my lady
was stricken with its cruelty;
because the delight of her loveliness,
departing from our sight,
became a great spiritual beauty;
this beauty spreads through heaven
the light of love, which greets the angels
and makes their lofty, subtle intelligence
marvel, it is so noble.

XXXIV. On the day which completed a year since that lady had become one of the partakers of the eternal life, I was seated in a place where, remembering her, I was drawing an angel on certain tablets; and while I was drawing him, I turned my eyes and saw beside me men whom it was fitting to honor. They were looking at what I was doing; and as I was told later, they had been there a while before I noticed them. When I saw them, I stood up, and said in greeting: "Someone was with me just now, and that is why I was lost in thought." So that, after they left, I returned to my task; that is, drawing figures of angels; and, doing this, I had the idea of composing a poem, for the anniversary, as it were, and writing to those who had come to see me; and then I wrote this sonnet, which begins: "There had come to my mind." It has two different opening quatrains, so I shall analyze it with each of these in mind.

Well, then, with regard to the first opening, this sonnet has three parts: in the first, I say the lady was already in my memory; in the second, I say what Love did to me for that reason; in the third, I speak of the effects of Love. The second begins with the words "Love, who"; the third, with "They tearfully issued forth." This part is subdivided in two: in the first, I state that all my sighs came forth speaking; in the second, I state that some of them uttered certain words that were different from what the others said. The second begins with the words "But those." The same analysis is valid when the variant opening is used, except that in the first part I tell when that lady had thus come to my memory, which I do not state in the first version.

Primo cominciamento.

Era venuta ne la mente mia
    la gentil donna che per suo valore
    fu posta da l'altissimo signore
    nel ciel de l'umiltate, ov'è Maria.

Secondo cominciamento.

Era venuta ne la mente mia
    quella donna gentil cui piange Amore,
    entro 'n quel punto che lo suo valore
    vi trasse a riguardar quel ch'eo facia.
Amor, che ne la mente la sentia,
    s'era svegliato nel destrutto core,
    e diceva a'sospiri: «Andate fore»;
    per che ciascun dolente si partia.
Piangendo uscivan for de lo mio petto
    con una voce che sovente mena
    la lagrime dogliose a li occhi tristi.
Ma quei che n'uscian for con maggior pena,
    venian dicendo: «Oi nobile intelletto,
    oggi fa l'anno che nel ciel salisti».

XXXV. Poi per alquanto tempo, con ciò fosse cosa che io fosse in
parte ne la quale mi ricordava del passato tempo, molto stava pensoso,
e con dolorosi pensamenti, tanto che mi faceano parere de fore una
vista di terribile sbigottimento. Onde io, accorgendomi del mio
travagliare, levai li occhi per vedere se altri mi vedesse. Allora vidi una
gentile donna giovane e bella molto, la quale da una finestra mi
riguardava sì pietosamente, quanto a la vista, che tutta la pietà parea
in lei accolta. Onde, con ciò sia cosa che quando li miseri veggiono di
loro compassione altrui, più tosto si muovono a lagrimare, quasi come
di se stessi avendo pietade, io senti'allora cominciare li miei occhi a
volere piangere; e però, temendo di non mostrare la mia vile vita, mi
partio dinanzi da li occhi di questa gentile; e dicea poi fra me mede-
simo: «E' non puote essere che con quella pietosa donna non sia no-
bilissimo amore». E però proposi di dire uno sonetto, ne lo quale io
parlasse a lei, e conchiudesse in esso tutto ciò che narrato è in questa
ragione. E però che per questa ragione è assai manifesto, sì nollo di-
viderò. Lo sonetto comincia: *Videro li occhi miei.*

Videro li occhi miei quanta pietate
    era apparita in la vostra figura,

First Opening.
There had come to my mind
  the noble lady who for her worth
  had been placed by the Lord on high
  in the heaven of humility, where Mary is.

Variant Opening.
There had come to my mind
  that noble lady whom Love laments,
  at that moment when her worth
  induced you gentlemen to look at what I was doing.
  Love, who felt her in my mind,
  had awakened in my ravaged heart,
  and was saying to my sighs: "Go forth!"
  So that each one was departing in sorrow.
They tearfully issued forth from my breast
  with a sound that often brings
  the grieving tears to my sad eyes.
  But those which issued forth with greatest pain
  said as they came: "Ah, noble angel,
  today is a year since you ascended to heaven!"

XXXV. Then for some time, inasmuch as I was in a place that re-
minded me of the days past, I was very pensive, and my thoughts were
so sorrowful that they gave me an outward appearance of terrible dis-
may. Wherefore, remembering my suffering, I raised my eyes to see
whether anyone was looking at me. Then I saw a kindly young lady,
very beautiful, who was looking at me from a window so compassion-
ately, as it appeared, that all pity seemed to be gathered together in
her. And so, inasmuch as when the unfortunate see others pitying
them, they are more readily moved to tears, as if pitying themselves,
so to speak, I then felt my eyes to be on the verge of weeping; there-
fore, in fear of exhibiting the wretchedness of my life, I departed from
the sight of that kind lady, later saying to myself: "It is impossible that
that compassionate lady is devoid of most noble love." And so I re-
solved to write a sonnet in which I would address her, including in it
everything that has been narrated just now. And because the back-
ground is very obvious, I shall not analyze it. The sonnet begins: "My
eyes beheld."

My eyes beheld all the compassion
  that had appeared in your face

quando guardaste li atti e la statura
ch'io faccio per dolor molte fiate.
Allor m'accorsi che voi pensavate
la qualità de la mia vita oscura,
sì che mi giunse ne lo cor paura
di dimostrar con li occhi mia viltate.
E tolsimi dinanzi a voi, sentendo
che si movean le lagrime dal core,
ch'era sommosso da la vostra vista.
Io dicea poscia ne l'anima trista:
«Ben è con quella donna quello Amore
lo qual mi face andar così piangendo».

XXXVI. Avvenne poi che là ovunque questa donna mi vedea, sì si
facea d'una vista pietosa e d'un colore palido quasi come d'amore;
onde molte fiate mi ricordava de la mia nobilissima donna, che di si-
mile colore si mostrava tuttavia. E certo molte volte non potendo la-
grimare nè disfogare la mia tristizia, io andava per vedere questa pie-
tosa donna, la quale parea che tirasse le lagrime fuori de li miei occhi
per la sua vista. E però mi venne volontade di dire anche parole, par-
lando a lei, e dissi questo sonetto, lo quale comincia: *Color d'amore;*
ed è piano sanza dividerlo, per la sua precedente ragione.

Color d'amore e di pietà sembianti
non preser mai così mirabilmente
viso di donna, per veder sovente
occhi gentili o dolorosi pianti,
come lo vostro, qualora davanti
vedetevi la mia labbia dolente;
sì che per voi mi ven cosa a la mente,
ch'io temo forte non lo cor si schianti.
Eo non posso tener li occhi distrutti
che non reguardin voi spesse fiate,
per desiderio di pianger ch'elli hanno:
e voi crescete sì lor volontate,
che de la voglia si consuman tutti;
ma lagrimar dinanzi a voi non sanno.

XXXVII. Io venni a tanto per la vista di questa donna, che li miei
occhi si cominciaro a dilettare troppo di vederla; onde molte volte me
ne crucciava nel mio cuore ed aveamene per ville assai. Onde più
volte bestemmiava la vanitade de li occhi miei, e dicea loro nel mio

when you looked at the actions and attitude
that I frequently adopt out of sorrow.
Then I observed that you were thinking of
the nature of my obscure life,
so that the fear came to my heart
of exhibiting my baseness in my eyes.
And I removed myself from your sight, feeling
tears welling up from my heart,
which was moved by the sight of you.
Later, I said in my sad soul:
"Surely that Love is with that woman
which makes me go about weeping this way!"

XXXVI. It then befell that wherever that lady saw me, her face took
on a pitying expression and turned pale, almost as if with love; so that
I frequently recalled my very noble lady, who had constantly showed
herself with a similar coloring. And certainly many times, unable to
weep or relieve my sadness, I would go to look at that compassionate
lady, who seemed to draw the tears from my eyes at the very sight of
her. And so I felt the desire to write another poem addressing her, and
I wrote this sonnet, which begins: "Amorous pallor." Its meaning is
clear without analysis, from the account I have just given.

Amorous pallor and expressions of pity
never suffused so wondrously
a lady's face, upon frequently beholding
kindly eyes or sorrowful tears,
as they do yours, whenever you see
my grieving features before you;
so that, because of you, a thing comes to my mind
that I greatly fear will make my heart burst.
I cannot restrain my ravaged eyes
from beholding you often
because of the desire they have to weep:
and you augment their wishes so greatly
that they are fully consumed by that urge,
but are unable to weep in your presence.

XXXVII. The sight of that lady led me into such a state that my eyes
began to take too much pleasure in beholding her; so that frequently
I was tortured in my heart and held myself very cheaply. And so, I
often cursed the vanity of my eyes, saying to them in my mind: "You

pensero: «Or voi solavate fare piangere chi vedea la vostra dolorosa
condizione, e ora pare che vogliate dimenticarlo per questa donna che
vi mira; che non mira voi, se non in quanto le pesa de la gloriosa donna
di cui piangere solete; ma quanto potete fate, chè io la vi pur rimem-
brerò molto spesso, maladetti occhi, chè mai, se non dopo la morte,
non dovrebbero le vostre lagrime avere restate». E quando così avea
detto fra me medesimo a li miei occhi, e li sospiri m'assalivano gran-
dissimi e angosciosi. E acciò che questa battaglia che io avea meco
non rimanesse saputa pur dal misero che la sentia, propuosi di fare un
sonetto, e di comprendere in ello questa orribile condizione. E dissi
questo sonetto, lo quale comincia: *L'amaro lagrimar.* Ed hae due
parti: ne la prima parlo a li occhi miei sì come parlava lo mio cuore in
me medesimo; ne la seconda rimuovo alcuna dubitazione, manife-
stando chi è che così parla; e comincia questa parte quivi: *Così dice.*
Potrebbe bene ancora ricevere più divisioni, ma sariano indarno, però
che è manifesto per la precedente ragione.

> «L'amaro lagrimar che voi faceste,
>   oi occhi miei, così lunga stagione,
>   facea lagrimar l'altre persone
>   de la pietate, come voi vedeste.
> Ora mi par che voi l'obliereste,
>   s'io fosse dal mio lato sì fellone,
>   ch'i' non ven disturbasse ogne cagione,
>   membrandovi colei cui voi piangeste.
> La vostra vanità mi fa pensare,
>   e spaventami sì, ch'io temo forte
>   del viso d'una donna che vi mira.
> Voi non dovreste mai, se non per morte,
>   la vostra donna, ch'è morta, obliare.»
> Così dice 'l meo core, e poi sospira.

XXXVIII. Ricovrai la vista di quella donna in sì nuova condizione,
che molte volte ne pensava sì come di persona che troppo mi piacesse;
e pensava di lei così: «Questa è una donna gentile, bella, giovane e
savia, e apparita forse per volontade d'Amore, acciò che la mia vita si
riposi». E molte volte pensava più amorosamente, tanto che lo cuore
consentiva in lui, cioè nel suo ragionare. E quando io avea consentito
ciò, e io mi ripensava sì come da la ragione mosso, e dicea fra me
medesimo: «Deo, che pensero è questo, che in così vile modo vuole
consolare me e non mi lascia quasi altro pensare?». Poi si rilevava un
altro pensero, e diceame: «Or tu se' stato in tanta tribulazione, perchè

formerly reduced to tears everyone who saw your sorrowful state, and now it appears you want to forget this because of that lady who gazes at you; but she gazes at you merely because she is grieving for the lady in glory whom you used to lament. But do as much as you can, for I will still remind you of her frequently, accursed eyes, because your tears should never have been lacking, except when you were dead." And after I had thus addressed my eyes mentally, sighs assailed me that were mighty and extremely anguished. And so that this battle with myself should not be known solely by the wretch who felt it, I resolved to write a sonnet and to describe in it this horrible state of mind. And I wrote this sonnet, which begins: " 'The bitter tears.' " And it has two parts: in the first, I address my eyes, just as my heart spoke within me; in the second, I dispel some doubt by making it clear who is speaking in this way; and this part begins with the words "Thus speaks." It could be subdivided even further, but this would be needless because it is clear from the foregoing account.

> "The bitter tears that you have shed,
>   ah, my eyes, for so long a period
>   made other people weep
>   with pity, as you saw.
>   Now I think you would forget to do so,
>   were I so villainous on my part
>   as not to thwart you on every occasion,
>   reminding you of the woman you lamented.
> Your lack of purpose makes me brood,
>   and frightens me so, that I greatly fear
>   the face of a woman who gazes at you.
>   You should never, except in death,
>   forget your lady who has died."
> Thus speaks my heart, and then it sighs.

XXXVIII. I harbored the sight of that lady in such a new state of mind that I often thought of her as a person I liked all too well; and I thought of her like this: "She is a kind, lovely, young, and wise lady, who has perchance appeared by the will of Love, so that my life may find repose." And often I thought of her more lovingly, so much so that my heart concurred with him; that is, with his, Love's, reasoning. And when I had yielded that far, I had second thoughts, as if incited by rational considerations, and I would say to myself: "God, what thoughts are these, which try to comfort me in so base a manner and hardly allow me to think differently?" Then yet another thought would arise, telling me: "Now you

non vuoli tu ritrarre te da tanta amaritudine? Tu vedi che questo è uno spiramento d'Amore, che ne reca li disiri d'amore dinanzi, ed è mosso da così gentil parte com'è quella de li occhi de la donna che tanto pietosa ci s'hae mostrata». Onde io, avendo così più volte combattuto in me medesimo, ancora ne volli dire alquante parole; e però che la battaglia de'pensieri vinceano coloro che per lei parlavano, mi parve che si convenisse di parlare a lei; e dissi questo sonetto, lo quale comincia: *Gentil pensero;* e dico —gentile— in quanto ragionava di gentile donna, chè per altro era vilissimo.

In questo sonetto fo due parti di me, secondo che li miei pensieri erano divisi. L'una parte chiamo cuore, cioè l'appetito; l'altra chiamo anima, cioè la ragione; e dico come l'uno dice con l'altro. E che degno sia di chiamare l'appetito cuore, e la ragione anima, assai è manifesto a coloro a cui mi piace che ciò sia aperto. Vero è che nel precedente sonetto io fo la parte del cuore contra quella de li occhi, e ciò pare contrario di quello che io dico nel presente; e però dico che ivi lo cuore anche intendo per lo appetito, però che maggiore desiderio era lo mio ancora di ricordarmi de la gentilissima donna mia, che di vedere costei, avvegna che alcuno appetito n'avessi già, ma leggiero parea: onde appare che l'uno detto non è contrario a l'altro.

Questo sonetto ha tre parti: ne la prima comincio a dire a questa donna come lo mio desiderio si volge tutto verso lei; ne la seconda dico come l'anima, cioè la ragione, dice al cuore, cioè a lo appetito; ne la terza dico com'e'le risponde. La seconda parte comincia quivi: *L'anima dice;* la terza quivi: *Ei le risponde.*

> Gentil pensero che parla di vui
> sen vene a dimorar meco sovente,
> e ragiona d'amor sì dolcemente,
> che face consentir lo core in lui.
> L'anima dice al cor: «Chi è costui,
> che vene a consolar la nostra mente,
> ed è la sua vertù tanto possente,
> ch'altro penser non lascia star con nui?»
> Ei le risponde: «Oi anima pensosa,
> questi è uno spiritel novo d'amore,
> che reca innanzi me li suoi desiri;
> e la sua vita, e tutto 'l suo valore,
> mosse de li occhi di quella pietosa
> che si turbava de'nostri martìri».

have been in such tribulation; why do you not want to withdraw from such bitterness? You see that this is an inspiration of Love, who presents the desires of love to us, and it has its origin in such a noble place as the eyes of the lady who showed herself so compassionate to us." So that, having thus struggled with myself numerous times, I wanted to say a few words more; and because the battle of thoughts was being won by those which spoke on her behalf, I felt it was proper to address her; and I wrote this sonnet, which begins: "A noble thought." And I call it noble in so far as it referred to a noble lady; viewed otherwise, it was extremely base.

In this sonnet, I divide myself into two parts, to match the conflict in my thoughts. I call one part my heart; that is, carnal appetite; the other I call my soul; that is, my reason; and I tell how each addresses the other. And that it is proper to call the appetite "heart," and the reasoning powers "soul," is quite evident to those to whom I wish this matter to be revealed. It is true that in the preceding sonnet I take the heart's part in its opposition to the eyes, and this seems contrary to what I say in the present one; and so I explain that, there, I also identify the heart with the appetite, because I still had a greater desire to remember my most noble lady than to look at this new lady, although I already had some appetite for her, but seemingly a slight one; hence it is clear that one poem does not contradict the other.

This sonnet has three parts: in the first, I start to tell this lady that my desire is turned altogether toward her; in the second, I say what my soul (that is, my reason) says to my heart (that is, my appetite); in the third, I give the latter's reply to the former. The second part begins with the words "My soul says"; the third, with "It answers her."

A noble thought that speaks of you
comes to dwell with me often,
and talks of love so sweetly
that it makes my heart concur with it.
My soul says to my heart: "Who is this
who comes to comfort our mind,
and whose influence is so potent
that he lets no other thought remain with us?"
It answers her: "Ah, pensive soul,
it is a new sprite of love
who presents his desires to me;
and his life, and all his power,
arose from the eyes of that compassionate lady
who was so perturbed by our sufferings."

XXXIX. Contra questo avversario de la ragione si levoe un die, quasi ne l'ora de la nona, una forte imaginazione in me, che mi parve vedere questa gloriosa Beatrice con quelle vestimenta sanguigne co le quali apparve prima a li occhi miei; e pareami giovane in simile etade in quale io prima la vidi. Allora cominciai a pensare di lei; e ricordandomi di lei secondo l'ordine del tempo passato, lo mio cuore cominciò dolorosamente a pentere de lo desiderio a cui sì vilmente s'avea lasciato possedere alquanti die contra la costanzia de la ragione: e discacciato questo cotale malvagio desiderio, sì si rivolsero tutti li miei pensamenti a la loro gentilissima Beatrice. E dico che d'allora innanzi cominciai a pensare di lei sì con tutto lo vergognoso cuore, che li sospiri manifestavano ciò molte volte; però che tutti quasi diceano nel loro uscire quello che nel cuore si ragionava, cioè lo nome di quella gentilissima, e come si partio da noi. E molte volte avvenia che tanto dolore avea in sè alcuno penser, ch'io dimenticava lui e là dov'io era. Per questo raccendimento de'sospiri si raccese lo sollenato lagrimare in guisa che li miei occhi pareano due cose che disiderassero pur di piangere; e spesso avvenia che per lo lungo continuare del pianto, dintorno loro si facea uno colore purpureo, lo quale suole apparire per alcuno martirio che altri riceva. Onde appare che de la loro vanitade fuoro degnamente guiderdonati; sì che d'allora innanzi non potero mirare persona che li guardasse sì che loro potesse trarre a simile intendimento. Onde io, volendo che cotale desiderio malvagio e vana tentazione paresse distrutto, sì che alcuno dubbio non potessero inducere le rimate parole ch'io avea dette innanzi, propuosi di fare uno sonetto ne lo quale io comprendesse la sentenzia di questa ragione. E dissi allora: *Lasso! per forza di molti sospiri;* e dissi —lasso— in quanto mi vergognava di ciò, che li miei occhi aveano così vaneggiato.

Questo sonetto non divido, però che assai lo manifesta la sua ragione.

> Lasso! per forza di molti sospiri,
>   che nascon de'penser che son nel core,
>   li occhi son vinti, e non hanno valore
>   di riguardar persona che li miri.
>   E fatti son che paion due disiri
>   di lagrimare e di mostrar dolore,
>   e spesse volte piangon sì, ch'Amore
>   li 'ncerchia di corona di martìri.
> Questi penseri, e li sospir ch'eo gitto,

XXXIX. Against that adversary of my reason there arose in me one day, about the hour of nones, a vivid vision in which I thought I saw the late Beatrice wearing those blood-red robes in which she first appeared before my eyes; and she looked young to me, the same age she was when I first saw her. Then I began to think of her; and remembering her in the chronological sequence of the past, my heart began to feel painfully repentant for the desire by which it had so basely allowed itself to be possessed for some days in opposition to the constancy of my rational powers; and that evil desire having been dislodged, all my thoughts reverted to their most noble Beatrice. And I say that, from then on, I began to think of her so hard with all my shame-laden heart that my sighs made it clear many a time; because they almost all said, as they issued forth, what was being spoken in my heart; that is, the name of that most noble lady, and how she departed from us. And it befell many a time that some of my thoughts brought such sorrow with them that I forgot them and where I was. Through this rekindling of my sighs my tears, temporarily stilled, were also so freshly stimulated that my eyes resembled two objects which desired to weep constantly; and it often came about that, because of the long continuation of my weeping, a purple ring formed around them, the kind that usually appears when a person endures some suffering. From which it is clear that they were duly repaid for their flighty glances; so that, from then on, they were unable to behold anyone who looked at them and be led into a similar intention. Hence, wishing that evil desire and idle temptation to seem destroyed, so that no doubt could be produced by the poems I had written previously, I resolved to write a sonnet in which I would give the meaning of this train of reasoning. And then I wrote: "Alas! by the force of many sighs." And I said "Alas!" because I was ashamed that my eyes had strayed in that fashion.

I do not analyze this sonnet because its background makes it quite clear.

Alas! by the force of many sighs,
    which arise from the thoughts in my heart,
    my eyes are overcome, and do not have the strength
    to look at anyone who beholds them.
    And they are in such a state that they resemble two desires
    of weeping and displaying grief,
    and often they cry so hard that Love
    encircles them with a martyr's crown.
These thoughts, and the sighs I utter,

diventan ne lo cor sì angosciosi,
ch'Amor vi tramortisce, sì lien dole;
però ch'elli hanno in lor li dolorosi
quel dolce nome di madonna scritto,
e de la morte sua molte parole.

XL. Dopo questa tribulazione avvenne, in quello tempo che molta
gente va per vedere quella imagine benedetta la quale Iesu Cristo la-
sciò a noi per essemplo de la sua bellissima figura, la quale vede la mia
donna gloriosamente, che alquanti peregrini passavano per una via la
quale è quasi mezzo de la cittade ove nacque e vivette e morio la gen-
tilissima donna. Li quali peregrini andavano, secondo che mi parve,
molto pensosi; ond'io, pensando a loro, dissi fra me medesimo:
«Questi peregrini mi paiono di lontana parte, e non credo che anche
udissero parlare di questa donna, e non ne sanno neente; anzi li loro
penseri sono d'altre cose che di queste qui, chè forse pensano de li
loro amici lontani, li quali noi non conoscemo». Poi dicea fra me
medesimo: «Io so che s'elli fossero di propinquo paese, in alcuna vista
parrebbero turbati passando per lo mezzo de la dolorosa cittade». Poi
dicea fra me medesimo: «Se io li potesse tenere alquanto, io li pur
farei piangere anzi ch'elli uscissero di questa cittade, però che io direi
parole le quali farebbero piangere chiunque le intendesse». Onde,
passati costoro da la mia veduta, propuosi di fare uno sonetto, ne lo
quale io manifestasse ciò che io avea detto fra me medesimo; e acciò
che più paresse pietoso, propuosi di dire come se io avesse parlato a
loro; e dissi questo sonetto, lo quale comincia: *Deh peregrini che pen-
sosi andate.* E dissi —peregrini— secondo la larga significazione del
vocabulo; chè peregrini si possono intendere in due modi, in uno largo
e in uno stretto: in largo, in quanto è peregrino chiunque è fuori de la
sua patria; in modo stretto non s'intende peregrino se non chi va verso
la casa di sa'Iacopo o riede. E però è da sapere che in tre modi si chia-
mano propriamente le genti che vanno al servigio de l'Altissimo: chia-
mansi palmieri in quanto vanno oltremare, là onde molte volte recano
la palma; chiamansi peregrini in quanto vanno a la casa di Galizia,
però che la sepultura di sa'Iacopo fue più lontana de la sua patria che
d'alcuno altro apostolo; chiamansi romei in quanto vanno a Roma, là
ove questi cu'io chiamo peregrini andavano.
    Questo sonetto non divido, però che assai lo manifesta la sua ra-
gione.

become so oppressive in my heart
that Love swoons there, he is so sorry for them;
because they have written on them, those sad ones,
that sweet name of my lady
and many words concerning her death.

XL. After that tribulation, it came about, in that season when many people go to see that blessed image which Jesus Christ left us as a semblance of his most beautiful face,[25] which my lady beholds in glory, that some pilgrims were walking down a street almost at the center of the city where that most noble lady was born, lived, and died. Those pilgrims, as it seemed to me, were lost in thought; so that, thinking of them, I said to myself: "These pilgrims seem to me to have come from afar, and I do not think they have even heard tell of that lady, but know nothing about her; rather, their thoughts are of other matters than our local ones, for perhaps they are thinking of their far-away friends, whom we do not know." Then I said to myself: "I know that if they were from a nearby place, in some way they would appear upset when walking through the center of the sorrowing city." Then I said to myself: "If I could detain them a little, I would make them, too, weep before they had left this city, because I would speak words that would make any listener weep." And so, after they had passed from my sight, I resolved to write a sonnet in which I would make manifest what I had said to myself; and in order for it to seem more pity-provoking, I resolved to write as if I were addressing them; and I wrote this sonnet, which begins: "O pilgrims who walk lost in thoughts." And I said "pilgrims" in the broader meaning of the word; because "pilgrim" can be understood in two senses, a broad one and a restricted one: in the broad sense, it applies to anyone who is outside his native area; in the strict sense, no one is truly a pilgrim who is not headed for the church of Santiago in Compostela, or returning from there. And so it should be known that those who wander in the service of the Most High have three proper appellations: they are called palmers if they go overseas, from where they often bring back palm leaves; they are called pilgrims if they go to the church in Galicia, because the tomb of Saint James was more distant from his homeland than that of any other apostle; they are called *romei* if they go to Rome, where those whom I here call pilgrims were headed.

I do not analyze this sonnet because its background discussion makes it quite clear.

---

25. Veronica's veil, displayed in Rome during Easter Week.

> Deh peregrini che pensosi andate,
>> forse di cosa che non v'è presente,
>> venite voi da sì lontana gente,
>> com'a la vista voi ne dimostrate,
>> che non piangete quando voi passate
>> per lo suo mezzo la città dolente,
>> come quelle persone che neente
>> par che 'ntendesser la sua gravitate?
> Se voi restate per volerlo audire,
>> certo lo cor de'sospiri mi dice
>> che lagrimando n'uscirete pui.
>> Ell'ha perduta la sua beatrice;
>> e le parole ch'om di lei pò dire
>> hanno vertù di far piangere altrui.

XLI. Poi mandaro due donne gentili a me pregando che io mandasse loro di queste mie parole rimate; onde io, pensando la loro nobilitade, propuosi di mandare loro e di fare una cosa nuova, la quale io mandasse a loro con esse, acciò che più onorevolemente adempiesse li loro prieghi. E dissi allora uno sonetto, lo quale narra del mio stato, e manda'lo a loro co lo precedente sonetto accompagnato, e con un altro che comincia: *Venite a intender*.

Lo sonetto lo quale io feci allora, comincia: *Oltre la spera;* lo quale ha in sè cinque parti. Ne la prima dico ove va lo mio pensero, nominandolo per lo nome d'alcuno suo effetto. Ne la seconda dico perchè va là suso, cioè chi lo fa così andare. Ne la terza dico quello che vide, cioè una donna onorata là suso; e chiamolo allora —spirito peregrino,— acciò che spiritualmente va là suso, e sì come peregrino lo quale è fuori de la sua patria, vi stae. Ne la quarta dico come elli la vede tale, cioè in tale qualitade, che io no lo posso intendere, cioè a dire che lo mio pensero sale ne la qualitade di costei in grado che lo mio intelletto no lo puote comprendere; con ciò sia cosa che lo nostro intelletto s'abbia a quelle benedette anime sì come l'occhio debole a lo sole: e ciò dice lo Filosofo nel secondo de la Metafisica. Ne la quinta dico che, avvegna che io non possa intendere là ove lo pensero mi trae, cioè a la sua mirabile qualitade, almeno intendo questo, cioè che tutto è lo cotale pensare de la mia donna, però ch'io sento lo suo nome spesso nel mio pensero: e nel fine di questa quinta parte dico —donne mie care,— a dare ad intendere che sono donne coloro a cui io parlo. La seconda parte comincia quivi: *intelligenza nova;* la terza quivi: *Quand'elli è giunto;*

O pilgrims who walk lost in thoughts
   of things, perhaps, that are not present before you,
   do you come from a place so distant,
   as you show in your appearance,
   that you fail to weep when you pass
   through the center of the sorrowing city,
   like people who in no way
   (it seems) understand its deep mourning?
If you wish to tarry and hear about it,
   my sighing heart assures me
   that you will then weep as you leave the city.
   It has lost its *beatrix*, the lady who made it blessed;
   and the words that can be said of her
   have the power to make strangers cry.

XLI. Then two gentlewomen sent to me asking me to send them some of these poems of mine; so that, in view of their nobility, I resolved to do so and to write something new which I would send to them along with those, in order to comply with their wishes more respectfully. And I then wrote a sonnet which describes my condition, and sent it to them accompanied by the foregoing sonnet and the earlier one beginning "Come hear."

The new sonnet I wrote on that occasion begins: "Beyond the sphere." It has five parts. In the first, I say where my thoughts are going, calling them by the name of one of their effects. In the second, I tell why they are going up there; that is, who is making them go there. In the third, I tell what they see; that is, a lady honored up there; and I then call them "pilgrim spirit," because they are going up there religiously and remaining there like a pilgrim away from his homeland. In the fourth, I tell how they see her in such a form—that is, in such a condition—that I cannot fathom it; that is to say, my thoughts ascend as they view her condition to a height that my intellect cannot grasp; inasmuch as our intellect stands in the same relation to those souls in bliss as our weak eyes do to the sun: the Philosopher says this in the second book of his *Metaphysics*. In the fifth part I say that, although I cannot understand everything my thoughts carry me up to—that is, her wondrous condition—this at least I do understand: that these thoughts are all of my lady, because I frequently hear her name in my thoughts. And at the end of this fifth part I say "my dear ladies" to indicate that it is ladies whom I am addressing. The second part begins with the words "a new intelligence";

la quarta quivi: *Vedela tal;* la quinta quivi: *So io che parla.*
Potrebbesi più sottilmente ancora dividere, e più sottilmente fare
intendere; ma puotesi passare con questa divisa, e però non m'in-
trametto di più dividerlo.

> Oltre la spera che più larga gira
>   passa 'l sospiro ch'esce del mio core:
>   intelligenza nova, che l'Amore
>   piangendo mette in lui, pur su lo tira.
>   Quand'elli è giunto là dove disira,
>   vede una donna, che riceve onore,
>   e luce sì, che per lo suo splendore
>   lo peregrino spirito la mira.
> Vedela tal, che quando 'l mi ridice,
>   io no lo intendo, sì parla sottile
>   al cor dolente, che lo fa parlare.
>   So io che parla di quella gentile,
>   però che spesso ricorda Beatrice,
>   sì ch'io lo 'ntendo ben, donne mie care.

XLII. Appresso questo sonetto apparve a me una mirabile visione,
ne la quale io vidi cose che mi fecero proporre di non dire più di
questa benedetta infino a tanto che io potesse più degnamente
trattare di lei. E di venire a ciò io studio quanto posso, sì com'ella sae
veracemente. Sì che, se piacere sarà di colui a cui tutte le cose vivono,
che la mia vita duri per alquanti anni, io spero di dicer di lei quello che
mai non fue detto d'alcuna. E poi piaccia a colui che è sire de la corte-
sia, che la mia anima se ne possa gire a vedere la gloria de la sua
donna, cioè di quella benedetta Beatrice, la quale gloriosamente mira
ne la faccia di colui *qui est per omnia secula benedictus.*

the third, with "When it has arrived"; and fourth, with "He sees her to be such"; the fifth, with "I know he speaks." It could be divided even more complexly, and expounded more subtly; but it can pass with this division, and so I do not linger over further analysis.

> Beyond the sphere with the broadest orbit[26]
>> the sigh passes that issues from my heart:
>> a new intelligence, which Love
>> tearfully bestows on it, draws it ever upward.
> When it has arrived where it desires,
>> it sees a lady, who is receiving honors,
>> and who is so radiant that by her glow
>> that pilgrim spirit is able to behold her.
> He sees her to be such that, when he reports it to me,
>> I fail to understand, so subtly he speaks
>> to my grieving heart, which bids him speak.
> I know he speaks of that noble lady,
>> because he frequently mentions Beatrice,
>> so that I understand it well, my dear ladies.

XLII. After I wrote that sonnet, a wondrous vision appeared to me, in which I saw things that made me resolve to speak no further of that blessed lady until I could discuss her in a worthier manner. And I am striving as best I can to reach that goal, as she truly knows. Therefore, if it will be the pleasure of the One in whom all things live that my life lasts a few years more, I hope to say of her that which has never yet been said of any woman. And then may it please the One who is lord of courtesy that my soul may be able to go and see the glory of its lady—that is, that blessed Beatrice—who in glory beholds the face of him "who is blessed through all eternity."

---

26. The ninth heaven (the Primum Mobile), past which the Empyrean is situated.

APPENDICE

Giacomo da Lentini

Or come pote sí gran donna entrare
    per gli occhi mei, che sí piccioli sone?
    e nel mio core come pote stare,
    che 'nentr'esso la porto laonque i'vone?
    Loco laonde entra già non pare,
    ond'io gran meraviglia me ne dòne;
    ma voglio lei a lumera asomigliare,
    e gli occhi mei al vetro ove si póne.
Lo foco inchiuso poi passa di fore
    lo suo lostrore, sanza far rottura:
    cosí per gli occhi mi pass'a lo core,
    no la persona, ma la sua figura.
    Rinovellare mi voglio d'amore,
    poi porto insegna di tal crïatura.

Bonagiunta Orbicciani

A me adovene com'a lo zitello
    quando lo foco davanti li pare,
    che tanto li risembla chiaro e bello,
    che stendive la mano per pigliare;
    e lo foco lo 'ncende, e fallo fello,
    ché non è gioco lo foco toccare:
    poi ch'è passata l'ira, alora e quello
    disïa inver'lo foco ritornare.
Ma eo, che traggo l'aigua de lo foco
    (e no è null'om che lo potesse fare),
    per lacrime ch'eo getto tutto coco,
    chiare e salse quant'è acqua di mare.

APPENDIX

Giacomo da Lentini

Now, how can so great a lady enter
   through my eyes, which are so small?
And how can she fit in my heart,
   which is where I carry her wherever I go?
A place by which she can enter is not to be seen,
   so that I am greatly amazed;
but I wish to liken her to a candle,
   and my eyes to the glass of the lantern it is in.
The enclosed flame then makes its glow
   pass outside without any breakage:
   thus, through my eyes there passes to my heart
   not the lady herself, but her image.
I want to become rejuvenated in love
   since I bear the banner of such a being.

Bonagiunta Orbicciani

It is with me as with a little boy
   when he sees a flame before him,
   which seems so bright and lovely to him
   that he holds out his hand to take it;
and the flame burns him, and makes him unhappy,
   because it is no joke to touch fire:
after his sorrow is past, then even he
   desires to return to the flame.
But I, who draw water from fire
   (and there is no one else who could do it),
   am all ablaze with the tears I shed,
   as bright and salty as sea water.

Candela che s'aprende senza foco,
arde ed incende e non si pò amortare.

Guittone d'Arezzo

Ahi Deo, chi vidde mai tal malatia
    di quella che sorpreso hame lo core?
    ché la cosa ch'altrui par venen sia
    è sola medicina al meo dolore.
    Ciò è l'amor, ch'ogni om ch'el signoria
    guaimenta e dice che per lui si more,
    e pur se pena di trovare via
    como de sé islocar possa l'amore.
Ed eo pur peno di condurlo a mene
    e di venir de sua corte servente
    perché disïo ciò piú ch'altro bene.
    Ma pur languisco, lasso, e mor'sovente,
    dapoi ch'ello di me cura non tene:
    adonque guarrea me l'altrui nocente.

Guido Guinizzelli

Vedut'ho la lucente stella diana,
    ch'apare anzi che 'l giorno rend'albore,
    c'ha preso forma di figura umana;
    sovr'ogn'altra me par che dea splendore:
    viso de neve colorato in grana,
    occhi lucenti, gai e pien'd'amore;
    non credo che nel mondo sia cristiana
    sí piena di biltate e di valore.
Ed io dal suo valor son assalito
    con sí fera battaglia di sospiri
    ch'avanti a lei de dir non seri'ardito.
    Cosí conoscess'ella i miei disiri!
    ché, senza dir, de lei seria servito
    per la pietà ch'avrebbe de'martiri.

Guido Cavalcanti

Veggio negli occhi de la donna mia
    un lume pien di spiriti d'amore,

A candle that ignites without fire
burns and blazes and cannot be extinguished.

Guittone d'Arezzo

Oh, God, who ever saw a sickness equal
   to the one which has caught my heart off guard?
   For that which seems to others to be poison
   is the only medicine for my pain.
   It is love, for every man it masters
   laments and says it is causing his death,
   and constantly strives to find a way
   to be able to rid himself of Love.
But I constantly strive to lead him to me
   and become a servant in his court
   because I desire this above all other benefits.
   Yet, alas, I constantly languish and frequently die,
   since he assumes no care for me:
   and so, what harms others would cure me.

Guido Guinizzelli

I have seen the bright morning star
   that appears before the day breaks;
   it has taken the shape of a human being,
   and seems to me to shine beyond all others:
   a face of snow with a flush of carmine,
   shining eyes that are merry and full of love;
   I do not think there is another woman in the world
   so full of beauty and worth.
And I am assailed by her worth
   in so fierce a battle of sighs
   that I would not dare to speak in her presence.
   How I wish she were aware of my desires!
   For, without speaking, I would be rewarded by her
   out of the pity she would feel for my sufferings.

Guido Cavalcanti

I see in my lady's eyes
   a light filled with spirits of love

che porta uno piacer novo nel core,
sí che vi desta d'allegrezza vita.
Cosa m'aven, quand'i'le son presente,
ch'i'no la posso a lo 'ntelletto dire:
veder mi par de la sua labbia uscire
una sí bella donna, che la mente
comprender no la può, che 'mmantenente
ne nasce un'altra di bellezza nova,
da la qual par ch'una stella si mova
e dica: "La salute tua è apparita."
Là dove questa bella donna appare
s'ode una voce che le vèn davanti
e par che d'umiltà il su'nome canti
sí dolcemente, che, s'i' 'l vo'contare,
sento che 'l su'valor mi fa tremare;
e movonsi nell'anima sospiri
che dicon: "Guarda; se tu coste'miri,
vedra'la sua vertú nel ciel salita."

Dante Alighieri

Guido, i'vorrei che tu e Lapo ed io
fossimo presi per incantamento
e messi in un vasel, ch'ad ogni vento
per mare andasse al voler vostro e mio;
sì che fortuna od altro tempo rio
non ci potesse dare impedimento,
anzi, vivendo sempre in un talento,
di stare insieme crescesse 'l disio.
E monna Vanna e monna Lagia poi
con quella ch'è sul numer de le trenta
con noi ponesse il buono incantatore:
e quivi ragionar sempre d'amore,
e ciascuna di lor fosse contenta,
sì come i'credo che saremmo noi.

Bicci novel, figliuol di non so cui,
s'i'non ne domandasse monna Tessa,
giù per la gola tanta roba hai messa,
ch'a forza ti convien torre l'altrui.

that brings a new delight to my heart,
so that it awakens a life of merriment there.
Something happens to me when I am with her
that I cannot explain rationally:
I seem to see issuing from her facial expression
a lady so beautiful that the mind
cannot comprehend her, for immediately
there springs from her another, of sublime beauty,
from whom a star seems to arise
and say: "Your salvation has appeared."
Where this beautiful woman appears,
a voice is heard preceding her
which seems to sing her name humbly
and so sweetly that, if I try to report it,
I feel that its power makes me tremble;
and sighs are stirred in my soul
that say: "Look; if you behold her,
you will see that her virtue has ascended to heaven."

Dante Alighieri

Guido, I wish that you and Lapo and I
were laid under a spell
and placed on a ship which with every wind
would sail the sea wherever you two and I wanted it to,
so that no tempest or other bad weather
could hinder us;
rather, as we constantly lived in the same frame of mind,
our desire to stay together would increase.
And Miss Vanna and Miss Lagia then,
along with lady number thirty,
would be placed there with us by the kindly sorcerer:
and there we would always speak love,
and each of those women would be contented,
just as I believe *we* would be.

Young Bicci, son of I know not what man
(unless I asked your mother Mis' Tessa),
you have flung so much stuff down your gullet
that you are compelled to steal from others.

E già la gente si guarda da lui,
chi ha borsa a lato, là dov'e's'appressa,
dicendo: «Questi c'ha la faccia fessa
è piuvico ladron negli atti sui».
E tal giace per lui nel letto tristo,
per tema non sia preso a lo 'mbolare,
che gli appartien quanto Giosepp'a Cristo.
Di Bicci e de'fratei posso contare
che, per lo sangue lor, del male acquisto
sanno a lor donne buon cognati stare.

And folks are already watching out for you,
   anyone with a purse at his side, wherever you approach,
   saying: "This fellow with the scarred face
   is a notorious thief in his behavior."
And a certain man is lying in bed sorrowing for you,
   fearing you will be caught stealing,
   who is no more your father than Saint Joseph was Christ's.
   Of Bicci and his brothers I can relate
   that, joined by blood, with their ill-gotten gains
   they know how to be good brothers-in-law to their wives.

ALPHABETICAL LIST OF ITALIAN FIRST LINES OF POEMS

In "La vita nuova"

In the Appendix